Ladies' Home Journal

Easy as 1-2-3

WARM WEATHER COOKBOOK

by the Editors of Ladies' Home Journal

PUBLISHED BY LADIES' HOME JOURNAL BOOKS

Ladies' Home Journal

Myrna Blyth, Editor-in-Chief
Sue B. Huffman, Food Editor
Jan T. Hazard, Associate Food Editor
Tamara Schneider, Art Director

Produced in association with Media Projects Incorporated

Carter Smith, Executive Editor
Ellen Coffey, Senior Project Editor
Donna Ryan, Project Editor
Bernard Schleifer, Design Consultant
Design by Bruce Glassman

Preface

I know, especially when the weather is pleasant, few of us want or are able to spend hours in the kitchen. But I think it's sad that just because we no longer have time to make elaborate meals, we rarely sit down together as a family to talk, joke, share the happenings of our day. And without this special time together, a lot that shouldn't be missed can be missed.

At Ladies' Home Journal *we think most families would like to get the family-meal habit back. How can it be done? Start with the meal and realize that preparing dinner* doesn't *have to be a wearying chore. For example, meals in our* Easy as 1-2-3 Warm Weather Cookbook *can all be made in thirty minutes or less. And the menus are so delectable we know that Dad will (gladly) trade in his leftovers, and the kids their reheated pizza, to share a delicious dinner that ends with a terrific dessert.*

On a warm night, sitting on the deck or porch enjoying a pleasant meal, a family can talk about past vacations, this year's plans, Grandpa and Grandma's visit, the home team's chances, the upcoming swim meet—until the cookies are eaten, the ice cream melted in the dish. There's nothing but reruns on TV anyway, so watching fireflies is a lot more interesting, and with the help of this Easy as 1-2-3 Warm Weather Cookbook, *your family is guaranteed a relaxing and flavor-filled end to a special day.*

Myrna Blyth
Editor-in-Chief
Ladies' Home Journal

Contents

Introduction

"If you can't stand the heat, stay out of the kitchen," Harry Truman was fond of saying. The problem is, we still have to eat, even in warm weather, and we can't cook out on the grill every night.

With our Easy as 1-2-3 Warm Weather Cookbook, Ladies' Home Journal proves you can keep your cool and still turn out tasty, nutritious meals. Some are no-cook, the rest are quick-cook, so you can be out of the kitchen in minutes (thirty, to be exact).

Become an instant hero(ine) to your gang by whipping out our Classic Heroes, or the Italian Sausage and Pepper version. Treat them to some down-home favorites like Southern Fried Catfish or a unique Fried Chicken Salad, inspired by New Orleans' favorite Creole cook Paul Prudhomme. Can't make it to the Atlantic coast this summer? You can still serve Easthampton-style Lobster Rolls, as well as Crab Cakes à la Maryland.

Get away from basic burger boredom by sampling some delicious innovations—Maui Burgers, Malibu Burgers, Burrito Burgers. And on those sweltering dog days when you can't stand even to turn on a burner, you can rely on Caesar of the Sea (the classic salad with tuna) or Crab Louis. We offer a selection of seasonal dessert favorites like Blueberry Tumble and Sangria Peaches, ice cream chillers like Strawberry Shortcake Sundaes, even a speedy Chocolate Mousse.

Now warm weather eating doesn't have to be humdrum eating, thanks to the Ladies' Home Journal Easy as 1-2-3 Warm Weather Cookbook.

Sue B. Huffman
Food Editor
Ladies' Home Journal

Roast Beef Salad

A NO-COOK DINNER WITH A COOLING BEVERAGE

This satisfying meal is largely a matter of artful arranging rather than cooking; make it look as pretty as possible. The Watermelon Coolers, blender quick and summer delicious, can also be as pretty as a picture—garnished with lemon and sprigs of fresh mint.

Menu for 4

- **Watermelon Coolers**
- **Chef's Roast Beef Salad**

Crusty Bread with Paprika Butter

Chocolate-Frosted Cake

SHOPPING LIST

- ☐ 4 cans lemon-lime soda
- ☐ 1 pound cooked roast beef, thinly sliced
- ☐ 1 pound fresh green beans
- ☐ 2 large ripe tomatoes
- ☐ 1 onion
- ☐ 1 lemon
- ☐ 1 head Bibb or Boston lettuce
- ☐ 1 bunch fresh mint
- ☐ 1 bunch fresh parsley
- ☐ 1 wedge watermelon (¼ melon)
- ☐ 1 loaf crusty bread
- ☐ 1 chocolate-frosted cake
- ☐ 1 8-ounce container sour cream

Have on Hand

- ☐ Salt
- ☐ Pepper
- ☐ Paprika
- ☐ Butter
- ☐ Capers
- ☐ Red wine vinegar
- ☐ Dijon mustard

SCHEDULE

1. Cook green beans.
2. Mix ¼ pound butter with 1 teaspoon paprika.
3. Prepare Chef's Roast Beef Salad.
4. Prepare Watermelon Coolers.

Watermelon Coolers

3½ cups diced watermelon,
        seeds removed
2   tablespoons lemon juice
1   cup crushed ice
12   ice cubes
4   cans lemon-lime soda
        Lemon slices for garnish
        Fresh mint sprigs for
        garnish

Combine watermelon, lemon juice and crushed ice in blender. Blend at low speed 10 to 15 seconds. Half fill 4 tall glasses with mixture. Add 3 ice cubes to each; fill with lemon-lime soda. Garnish with lemon slices and mint sprigs.

Chef's Roast Beef Salad

1   pound fresh green beans,
        trimmed
1   teaspoon salt, divided
1   head Bibb or Boston
        lettuce
1   pound cooked roast beef,
        thinly sliced
2   large ripe tomatoes, cut into
        wedges or slices
½   cup sour cream
¼   cup Dijon mustard
1   tablespoon red wine
        vinegar
1   tablespoon lemon juice
1   tablespoon grated onion

¼   teaspoon pepper
2   tablespoons capers,
        drained
        Fresh parsley sprigs

In medium saucepan cook beans in boiling water to cover with ½ teaspoon salt 5 to 7 minutes, until tender-crisp; drain. Plunge into cold water to cool; drain well. Line large platter with lettuce leaves. Arrange green beans, roast beef and tomatoes on lettuce.

In small bowl combine sour cream, mustard, vinegar, lemon juice, grated onion, remaining ½ teaspoon salt and pepper. Stir or whisk until smooth. Spoon into mound in center of salad platter. Garnish with capers and fresh parsley sprigs.

CAPERS AS FLAVOR ACCENT OR GARNISH

- *Add lively flavor to sliced tomatoes by serving them with Caper Mayonnaise: To 1 cup mayonnaise add 2 teaspoons capers, 1 tablespoon minced onion and 2 teaspoons lemon juice or red wine vinegar.*
- *Mix 1 tablespoon capers into stuffing for baked or broiled fish.*
- *Top lemon slices with capers and use to garnish veal cutlets, fish fillets, salmon steaks.*
- *Arrange pimiento strips and capers on top of deviled eggs.*

Southern Fried Catfish

QUICK-COOKING FISH FRY

Frozen catfish is now available in many parts of the country. If you can find this southern treat, grab it; if not, substitute another white-fleshed fish. Serve it with an extra-easy cole slaw and a refreshing summer fruit dessert.

Menu for 4

- **Southern Fried Catfish Corn on the Cob**
- **Tangy Cole Slaw**
- **Melon with Rum and Lime Sauce**

SHOPPING LIST

☐ 1   pound frozen catfish fillets or other white fish fillets
☐ 8   ears fresh corn
☐ 1½   pounds cabbage
☐ 2   medium red onions
☐ 1   large or 2 small cantaloupe or other melons
☐ 2   limes
☐ 1   bunch fresh mint
☐ 1   8-ounce container sour cream
☐   Light rum

Have on Hand
☐   Salt
☐   Pepper
☐   Ground red pepper

☐   Dillweed
☐   Yellow cornmeal
☐   Sugar
☐   Salad oil
☐   Cider vinegar

SCHEDULE

1. Prepare Melon with Rum and Lime Sauce; chill.
2. Prepare Tangy Cole Slaw.
3. Heat water for corn.
4. Prepare Southern Fried Catfish.
5. Cook corn.

Southern Fried Catfish

½ cup yellow cornmeal
1 teaspoon salt
⅛ teaspoon ground red pepper
⅛ teaspoon black pepper
1 pound frozen catfish fillets or other white fish fillets, partially thawed and cut into 2- by 3-inch pieces
   Salad oil

In pie plate or shallow dish combine cornmeal, salt, red and black pepper. Dredge fish pieces in cornmeal mixture, patting to coat on all sides. In large heavy skillet heat about ½ inch oil to 375° F. or until a small piece of bread sizzles when dropped in. Add fish fillets and fry until golden brown, about 4 minutes on each side. Drain on paper towels.

Tangy Cole Slaw

5 cups chopped green cabbage (about 1½ pounds)
2 medium red onions, sliced
½ cup sour cream
1 tablespoon cider vinegar
1 teaspoon dillweed
½ teaspoon pepper
½ teaspoon salt

In large bowl combine all ingredients. Toss until well coated.

Melon with Rum and Lime Sauce

1 large or 2 small cantaloupes or other melons
½ cup sugar
¼ cup water
1 teaspoon grated lime peel
⅓ cup light rum
¼ cup lime juice
   Fresh mint

Split and seed melon, scoop out flesh and cut into bite-size pieces. Transfer to serving bowl; cover and refrigerate. In small saucepan mix sugar and water and bring to a boil. Lower heat and simmer 5 minutes. Add lime peel and let cool to room temperature. Stir in rum and lime juice. Pour over melon chunks and chill until serving time. Garnish with mint.

TIPS FOR FRYING FISH

- *Cook fish in batches if necessary to avoid crowding, which can produce a limp coating.*
- *Reheat oil to ideal frying temperature between batches.*
- *Skim out any free-floating bits and pieces to prevent them from burning.*
- *Drain fried fish on paper towels to remove excess oil.*

Fried Chicken Salad

SUMMER PERFECTION

Here is a terrific way to use frozen breaded chicken pieces—cooked, then tossed with bacon in a salad studded with blue cheese. Cool off first with an icy pineapple drink and end the meal with an unusual ice cream dessert.

Menu for 6

- **Sparkling Pineapple Drink**
- **Fried Chicken Salad**
- **Sesame Italian Bread**
- **Apple Pie Sundaes**

SHOPPING LIST

- ☐ ½ pound bacon
- ☐ 1 large head iceberg lettuce
- ☐ 1 head romaine lettuce
- ☐ 2 tomatoes
- ☐ 1 onion
- ☐ 1 pint strawberries or 1 lime or fresh pineapple
- ☐ 1 quart pineapple juice
- ☐ 1 21-ounce can apple pie filling
- ☐ Cheddar cheese crackers
- ☐ Sesame Italian bread
- ☐ 1 12-ounce package frozen breaded drumstick-shaped chicken pieces
- ☐ 1 8-ounce container sour cream
- ☐ 2 ounces blue cheese
- ☐ 1 quart vanilla ice cream

Have on Hand
- ☐ Pepper
- ☐ Mayonnaise
- ☐ Club soda or seltzer water

SCHEDULE

1. Prepare chicken and cook bacon.
2. Prepare Fried Chicken Salad.
3. Prepare Sparkling Pineapple Drink.
4. Prepare Apple Pie Sundaes.

Sparkling Pineapple Drink

1 quart pineapple juice
  Club soda or seltzer water
  Ice cubes
  Strawberries, lime slices or
    pineapple chunks for
    garnish

Fill each of 6 glasses ⅔ full of pineapple juice. Add club soda or seltzer and ice cubes. Garnish with strawberry, lime slice or pineapple chunk.

Fried Chicken Salad

1 package (12 oz.) frozen
    breaded drumstick-
    shaped chicken pieces
4 slices bacon, cut into 1-
    inch pieces
8 cups torn iceberg lettuce
4 cups romaine lettuce, cut
    crosswise into ½-inch
    strips
2 tomatoes, cut into wedges
½ cup onion rings
½ cup mayonnaise
½ cup sour cream
¼ cup (2 oz.) crumbled blue
    cheese
⅛ teaspoon pepper

Prepare chicken according to package directions. Cook bacon until crisp; drain on paper towels. In large bowl combine lettuce, tomatoes and onion. In small bowl mix remaining ingredients; pour over salad and toss. Add chicken and bacon; toss again and serve immediately.

Apple Pie Sundae

1 quart vanilla ice cream
1 can (21 oz.) apple pie
    filling
  Cheddar cheese crackers,
    crushed

Place 2 small scoops ice cream in each dish. Spoon on apple pie filling and top with crushed crackers.

MORE COOL DRINKS FOR WARM EVENINGS

- Vegetable Coolers: *Whirl in blender 1½ cups vegetable juice cocktail, 8 ounces plain yogurt, ½ teaspoon celery salt, dash Worcestershire sauce and a few drops of red pepper sauce.*
- Black Cows: *Ease scoops of vanilla ice cream into tall glasses of root beer.*
- Orange Fluff: *Puree in blender 1 egg white, 1½ cups orange juice, ¾ cup milk, 5 ice cubes and 2 tablespoons sugar. Whirl until ice is crushed.*

Crab Louis

COOL AND CREAMY SEAFOOD PLATTER

Beautifully garnished lump crabmeat with a cream-and-vegetable dressing. What main dish could be more appropriate for a summer evening? Serve this delightful fresh blueberry dessert just barely warm.

Menu for 4

- **Crab Louis**
- **Broccoli Vinaigrette**
- **Hard Rolls**
- **Blueberry Tumble**

SHOPPING LIST

☐ 1	bunch broccoli	
☐ 1	head lettuce	
☐ 1	green pepper	
☐ 1	bunch fresh chives or 1 small package or jar dried chives	
☐ 1	bunch green onions	
☐ 2	tomatoes	
☐ 1	avocado	
☐ 1	lemon	
☐ 1	pint blueberries	
☐ 1	package hard rolls	
☐ 1	small package granola	
☐ 1	small can ripe olives	
☐ 1	small can or package flaked coconut	
☐ ½	pint heavy or whipping cream	
☐ 1	pound lump crabmeat	

☐   Cinnamon
☐   Sugar
☐   Butter or margarine
☐   Salad oil
☐   Cider vinegar
☐   Garlic
☐   Eggs
☐   Mayonnaise
☐   Chili sauce
☐   Bottled red pepper sauce

Have on Hand
☐   Salt
☐   Pepper

SCHEDULE

1. Prepare Broccoli Vinaigrette; chill.
2. Cook blueberries and set aside to cool.
3. Prepare Crab Louis.
4. Mix topping for Blueberry Tumble.

Crab Louis

Lettuce leaves
1   *pound lump crabmeat*
½   *cup mayonnaise*
2   *tablespoons heavy or*
        whipping cream
2   *tablespoons chili sauce*
1   *tablespoon lemon juice*
¼   *teaspoon red pepper sauce*
2   *tablespoons diced green*
        pepper
2   *minced green onions*
2   *tomatoes, cut into wedges*
8   *ripe olives*
1   *avocado, peeled and sliced*
2   *hard-cooked eggs, cut into*
        wedges

Line a large platter with lettuce leaves. Mound crabmeat in center. In small bowl stir together mayonnaise, cream, chili sauce, lemon juice, red pepper sauce, green pepper and onion. Spoon dressing around crabmeat. Garnish with olives, avocado and egg wedges.

Broccoli Vinaigrette

1   *bunch broccoli, trimmed*
1   *teaspoon salt*
½   *cup salad oil*
2   *tablespoons cider vinegar*
1   *garlic clove, crushed*
1   *tablespoon fresh chives or*
        1 teaspoon dried
⅛   *teaspoon pepper*

Plunge broccoli spears into salted boiling water; cook, uncovered, 10 to 12 minutes until broccoli is bright green and just tender. Drain and plunge into cold water to cool; drain well and transfer to serving dish.

In small jar with tight-fitting lid combine remaining ingredients. Pour dressing over broccoli and turn to coat. Refrigerate until serving time.

Blueberry Tumble

3   *cups blueberries*
2   *tablespoons sugar*
¼   *teaspoon cinnamon*
1   *cup granola*
½   *cup flaked coconut*
⅓   *cup melted butter or*
        margarine

In saucepan combine berries, sugar and cinnamon. Cook over low heat 15 minutes. Cool slightly and spoon into dessert dishes. In small bowl combine granola, coconut and melted butter or margarine; spoon over berries.

COOL CRABMEAT APPETIZER

Crab Cocktail: *Mix ¾ pound crabmeat with ½ cup chopped celery; mound on lettuce leaves and serve with cocktail sauce made from ¾ cup ketchup, ½ tablespoon prepared horseradish, 2 teaspoons lemon juice, pepper to taste and a dash of hot pepper sauce.*

Chicken in Lime Sauce

A COOL SUMMER ENTREE

Tangy limes and Dijon mustard add zip to this sauce, which is delicious with veal, pork or turkey as well as chicken. The fresh green beans get their crunch from sauteed almonds. Chocolate Mousse, a perennial favorite, is a perfect ending for almost any meal.

Menu for 4

- **Chicken in Lime Sauce**
  Green Beans with Almonds
- **Rice**
- **Chocolate Mousse**

SHOPPING LIST

- ☐ 4 chicken cutlets
- ☐ 1 pound fresh green beans
- ☐ 2 limes
- ☐ 1 13¾- or 14½-ounce can chicken broth
- ☐ 1 6-ounce package semisweet chocolate chips
- ☐ 1 small can or package slivered almonds
- ☐ ½ pint heavy or whipping cream

- ☐ Long-grain rice
- ☐ Cornstarch
- ☐ Instant coffee
- ☐ Butter or margarine
- ☐ Eggs
- ☐ Dijon mustard
- ☐ Vanilla extract

Have on Hand

- ☐ Salt
- ☐ Pepper
- ☐ Sugar
- ☐ Brown sugar

SCHEDULE

1. Prepare Chocolate Mousse; chill in freezer.
2. Cook rice.
3. Prepare green beans with almonds.
4. Prepare Chicken in Lime Sauce.

Chicken with Lime Sauce

4   *chicken cutlets*
⅛   *teaspoon salt*
    Dash pepper
4   *tablespoons butter or margarine, divided*
¾   *cup chicken broth*
3   *tablespoons fresh lime juice, divided*
2   *teaspoons Dijon mustard*
1   *tablespoon brown sugar*
1   *teaspoon cornstarch*
¼   *cup water*

Pound chicken ¼-inch thick and season with salt and pepper. In heavy skillet melt 2 tablespoons butter or margarine over medium heat. Add chicken and saute about 3 minutes on each side. Transfer to platter, cover and set aside. Add broth, 2 tablespoons lime juice, mustard and brown sugar to skillet, scraping up browned bits. In small bowl combine cornstarch and water. Add to skillet; whisk over high heat until thickened, about 1 minute. Remove from heat. Whisk in remaining lime juice and butter, stirring until butter melts. Add chicken to skillet and heat through, turning to coat both sides with sauce. Do not boil.

Chocolate Mousse

2   *tablespoons sugar*
⅓   *cup water*
1   *teaspoon instant coffee*
1   *package (6 oz.) semisweet chocolate chips*
2   *eggs*
1   *teaspoon vanilla extract*
1   *cup heavy or whipping cream, whipped*

In small saucepan combine sugar, water and coffee; cook over medium heat until sugar dissolves, about 3 minutes. Combine with chocolate chips in blender; blend until smooth, stopping machine once or twice to scrape sides. Add eggs and vanilla and blend until smooth. Fold chocolate mixture into whipped cream. Spoon into serving dishes and chill in freezer until serving time.

QUICK FLAVOR WITH INSTANT COFFEE

- *Dissolve 1 teaspoon coffee granules or powder in equal amount of water. Shake with 1 can shredded coconut; sprinkle on cupcakes or ice cream.*
- *Blend into cake, pudding or frosting mix—vanilla becomes coffee flavor; chocolate becomes mocha.*
- *Cream a small amount with honey and butter and serve on French toast, pancakes or waffles.*

Neptune Salad

SUMMERY SEAFOOD WITH A FRUITY WINE DRINK

Quick and easy to assemble, yet special enough to serve at a party, this meal is sure to become a warm weather favorite. Serve the salad with white wine sangria and a dessert of pears marinated in sherry.

Menu for 4

- **Blond Sangria Baguette-Style French Bread**
- **Neptune Salad**
- **Pears Antoine with Sherbet**

SHOPPING LIST

- ☐ ½ pound cooked medium shrimp
- ☐ ½ pound cooked lobster meat
- ☐ 1 6-ounce package frozen crabmeat
- ☐ 1 tomato
- ☐ 1 bunch watercress
- ☐ 1 seedless orange
- ☐ 1 lemon
- ☐ 1 lime
- ☐ 3 fresh pears
- ☐ 1 2-ounce jar red salmon caviar
- ☐ 1 baguette
- ☐ 1 8-ounce container sour cream
- ☐ 1 pint lemon sherbet

Have on Hand

- ☐ Sugar
- ☐ Horseradish
- ☐ Mayonnaise
- ☐ Sherry
- ☐ Brandy
- ☐ Orange-flavored liqueur
- ☐ Dry white wine
- ☐ Club soda or seltzer water

SCHEDULE

1. Place wine and club soda in freezer to chill; mix remaining sangria ingredients and set aside.
2. Peel, core and slice pears; add sherry; refrigerate.
3. Prepare Neptune Salad.
4. Mix Blond Sangria.

Blond Sangria

1   seedless orange, thinly
       sliced
1   lime, thinly sliced
2   tablespoons sugar
¹/₃   cup orange-flavored
       liqueur
¹/₃   cup brandy
1   bottle dry white wine,
       chilled
2   cups club soda or seltzer,
       chilled
       Ice cubes

In pitcher combine orange and lime slices, sugar, liqueur and brandy. Let stand at room temperature until serving time. Pour wine and club soda into pitcher and stir. Serve over ice.

Neptune Salad

¹/₂   cup sour cream
¹/₄   cup mayonnaise
1   jar (2 oz.) red salmon
       caviar
2   teaspoons horseradish
¹/₂   pound shelled medium
       shrimp, cooked
¹/₂   pound cooked lobster meat
       cut into ¹/₂-inch chunks
1   package (6 oz.) frozen
       crabmeat, thawed and
       well drained, cut into
       ¹/₂-inch chunks
1   bunch watercress
1   large tomato, cut into 8
       wedges

In medium bowl combine sour cream, mayonnaise, caviar and horseradish. Add seafood and stir gently to coat well. Line serving dish with watercress and spoon salad on top. Garnish with tomato.

Pears Antoine with Sherbet

3   fresh pears
6   tablespoons sherry
1   pint lemon sherbet
2   tablespoons grated lemon
       peel

Peel and core pears; slice into chunks. Pour sherry into small bowl, add pears and marinate in refrigerator until serving time. Place 1 scoop sherbet in each of 4 dessert dishes. Spoon pear mixture on top and garnish with grated lemon peel.

RED SANGRIA

Combine ³/₄ cup each sugar and water. Bring to a boil and cook 3 to 4 minutes; cool. Add 1 sliced orange and 1 sliced lemon; let stand. Mix with 3 cups each dry red wine and club soda. Add dash of cognac, ice cubes and sliced peaches.

Nouvelle Chicken Breasts

LIGHT AND EASY DINING

This chicken entree is quick and easy, yet festive enough to serve to guests. Serve it accompanied by fluffy rice and a crisp salad of fresh green beans. On festive occasions serve the Chocolate Strawberries in paper bonbon cups.

Menu for 4

- **Nouvelle Chicken Breasts**
- **Fresh Green Bean Salad**
- **Rice**
- **Chocolate Strawberries**

SHOPPING LIST

- ☐ 4 chicken cutlets
- ☐ 1 pound fresh green beans
- ☐ 2 tomatoes
- ☐ 1 pint fresh strawberries
- ☐ 1 12-ounce package semisweet chocolate chips
- ☐ 1 7-ounce can hearts of palm
- ☐ 1 small jar green peppercorns
- ☐ ½ pint heavy or whipping cream

- ☐ Butter or margarine
- ☐ Garlic
- ☐ Salad oil
- ☐ Tarragon vinegar
- ☐ Red wine vinegar

Have on Hand
- ☐ Salt
- ☐ Pepper
- ☐ Dried tarragon
- ☐ Long-grain rice

SCHEDULE

1. Prepare Chocolate Strawberries; refrigerate.
2. Cook rice and green beans.
3. Assemble Fresh Green Bean Salad.
4. Prepare Chicken Breasts Nouvelle.

Nouvelle Chicken Breasts

4   *chicken cutlets*
½   *teaspoon salt*
⅛   *teaspoon pepper*
2   *tablespoons butter or margarine*
1   *tablespoon tarragon vinegar*
1   *tablespoon green peppercorns*
½   *cup heavy or whipping cream*

Preheat oven to 200° F. Between sheets of wax paper pound chicken ¼-inch thick. Sprinkle with salt and pepper.

In large skillet heat butter or margarine over medium-high heat. Add chicken and saute 3 minutes on each side. Keep warm in oven. Add vinegar and peppercorns to skillet and cook over medium-high heat for 1 minute, stirring. Add cream and continue cooking for 3 minutes, stirring occasionally. Pour over chicken.

Fresh Green Bean Salad

1   *pound green beans, trimmed*
¼   *cup salad oil*
¼   *cup red wine vinegar*
½   *teaspoon dried tarragon, crumbled*
1   *small garlic clove, crushed*
½   *teaspoon salt*
⅛   *teaspoon pepper*
2   *tomatoes, cut in wedges*

1   *can (7 oz.) hearts of palm, drained and quartered*

Cook green beans in boiling salted water 7 to 10 minutes, until just tender-crisp. Drain and plunge into cold water; drain well. In jar with tight-fitting lid combine oil, vinegar, tarragon, garlic, salt and pepper.

Arrange green beans, tomato wedges and hearts of palm on salad plate. Pour over dressing. Cover and chill until serving time.

Chocolate Strawberries

1   *pint fresh strawberries*
1   *package (12 oz.) semisweet chocolate chips*

Rinse strawberries but leave stems intact; dry well on paper towels. Melt chocolate bits in double boiler over hot but not boiling water. Stir until smooth; reduce heat to low. Dip berries in chocolate, one at a time, leaving an uncoated rim around the stem. Shake off excess chocolate; place berries on wax paper. Refrigerate about 30 minutes until set.

WHOLE FRESH STRAWBERRIES

- *Top them with sweetened sour cream dusted with brown sugar.*
- *Sprinkle with sugar and kirsch or fruit-flavored brandy.*
- *Serve in stemmed glasses of champagne.*

Sour Cream Hamburgers

A SATISFYING SUMMER COMBINATION

Hamburgers, sliced tomatoes, corn on the cob and ripe peaches make a perfect summer meal. These burgers are topped with a piquant sour cream sauce, and the corn is accompanied by a spicy butter.

Menu for 4

- **Sour Cream Hamburgers Sliced Tomatoes**
- **Corn on the Cob with Chili-Lime Butter**
- **Peach Passion**

SHOPPING LIST

- ☐ 2 large tomatoes
- ☐ 8 ears fresh corn
- ☐ 1 lime
- ☐ 4 large fresh peaches
- ☐ 1 bunch parsley
- ☐ 1 8-ounce container sour cream
- ☐ 1 pound ground beef

Have on Hand
- ☐ Salt
- ☐ Pepper
- ☐ Chili powder
- ☐ All-purpose flour
- ☐ Milk
- ☐ Butter or margarine
- ☐ Orange juice
- ☐ Dry red wine

SCHEDULE

1. Prepare Peach Passion; refrigerate.
2. Prepare Lime Butter.
3. Heat water for corn.
4. Cook Sour Cream Hamburgers.
5. Cook corn.
6. Slice tomatoes.

Sour Cream Hamburgers

1   *pound ground beef*
³/₄ *teaspoon salt*
¹/₈ *teaspoon pepper*
2   *tablespoons butter or*
        margarine
1   *tablespoon flour*
¹/₂ *cup milk*
¹/₂ *cup sour cream*
2   *tablespoons chopped*
        parsley

Season ground beef with salt and pepper and shape into 4 patties. In heavy skillet melt butter or margarine over medium heat; cook patties until browned, about 3 minutes on each side. Remove from skillet and set aside. Add flour to drippings in skillet and stir until smooth. Cook 1 minute more. Pour in milk and whisk until mixture comes to a boil. Return patties to skillet; cover and simmer over low heat 10 to 15 minutes. Transfer to serving platter. Remove skillet from heat; stir in sour cream. Pour sauce over patties. Garnish with parsley.

Corn on the Cob with Chili-Lime Butter

¹/₂ *cup butter or margarine,*
        softened
1   *tablespoon fresh lime juice*

1   *teaspoon chili powder*
¹/₂ *teaspoon salt*
8   *ears fresh corn, husked*

In small bowl thoroughly blend butter or margarine with lime juice. Add chili powder and salt; stir well.

Heat large pot of water to boiling. Add corn and cover. Return water to boil; cook 3 to 5 minutes. Drain well and serve with lime butter.

Peach Passion

4   *large fresh peaches*
³/₄ *cup dry red wine*
¹/₂ *cup orange juice*

Peel and pit peaches; cut into bite-size chunks. In serving bowl combine with wine and orange juice. Marinate in refrigerator until serving time.

STORING AND FREEZING GROUND BEEF

- *Store in coldest part of refrigerator, wrapped tightly in plastic wrap, up to 2 days.*
- *If not using meat within 2 days, shape into patties, wrap well and freeze up to 3 months.*
- *Label and date package before freezing.*

Stir-Fried Lean Pork Strips

PORK WITH GREEN BEANS, CHINESE STYLE

Stir-frying lets you cook quickly, allowing the foods to retain their natural goodness. Use fresh green beans, if you wish; blanch them quickly and drain well before adding to the wok or skillet.

Menu for 4

- **Stir-Fried Lean Pork Strips Rice**
- **Red and Gold Salad**
- **Trail Mix Sundaes**

SHOPPING LIST

- ☐ ½ pound lean boned pork shoulder
- ☐ ¼ pound fresh mushrooms
- ☐ 1 head Bibb or Boston lettuce
- ☐ 1 medium red onion
- ☐ 1 20-ounce bag frozen green beans
- ☐ 1 11-ounce can mandarin oranges
- ☐ 1 small package trail mix with dried fruit
- ☐ 1 pint frozen tofu-based dessert

Have on Hand
- ☐ Salt
- ☐ Pepper
- ☐ Dry mustard
- ☐ Dried basil (optional)

- ☐ Sugar
- ☐ Honey
- ☐ Long-grain rice
- ☐ Garlic
- ☐ Salad oil
- ☐ White wine vinegar
- ☐ Soy sauce
- ☐ Ground red pepper
- ☐ Dry sherry

SCHEDULE

1. Cook rice.
2. Prepare salad and dressing.
3. Cook Stir-Fried Lean Pork Strips.
4. Prepare Trail Mix Sundaes.

Stir-Fried Lean Pork Strips

½ pound lean boned pork
    shoulder, cut into 1-inch
    strips
2 tablespoons soy sauce,
    divided
1 garlic clove, minced
⅛ teaspoon ground red pepper
1 tablespoon dry sherry
½ teaspoon sugar
2 tablespoons salad oil,
    divided
1 cup sliced fresh mush-
    rooms (about ¼ lb.)
1 cup frozen green beans,
    thawed in cold water

In small bowl combine pork, 1 tablespoon soy sauce, garlic and red pepper; set aside. In another bowl combine remaining soy sauce, sherry and sugar.

In wok or medium skillet heat 1 tablespoon oil over medium high heat until hot but not smoking. Add pork and stir-fry until meat loses its pink color, about 4 minutes; remove pork. Add remaining oil to skillet and heat. Add mushrooms and green beans; stir-fry 3 minutes, until vegetables are tender but still crisp. Return pork to skillet; stir in sherry mixture. Cook 1 minute, or until hot and bubbly.

Red and Gold Salad

3 tablespoons salad oil

1 tablespoon white wine vinegar
⅛ teaspoon dry mustard
    Pinch dried basil
¼ teaspoon salt
⅛ teaspoon pepper
1 head Bibb or Boston let-
    tuce, torn
1 red onion, thinly sliced
    and separated into rings
½ cup mandarin oranges,
    drained

In measuring cup combine oil, vinegar, mustard, basil, salt and pepper. In salad bowl combine lettuce and onion rings; toss. Drizzle dressing over salad, add oranges and toss again.

Trail Mix Sundaes

1 pint frozen tofu-based
    dessert
½ cup trail mix with dried
    fruit, divided
¼ cup honey, divided

Place 1 scoop frozen tofu-based dessert in each of 4 dessert dishes. Sprinkle with 2 tablespoons trail mix. Drizzle with 1 tablespoon honey.

RICE TIPS

• *When cooking rice, your best bet is to follow package directions to the letter; each type of rice requires a different procedure.*
• *In general do not rinse; rinsing washes away some of the nutrients.*
• *Measure ingredients precisely.*

Malibu Burgers

AVOCADO BURGERS WITH FRESH TOMATO SALAD

Burgers, avocados, alfalfa sprouts and whole wheat pitas are the centerpiece of this laid-back West Coast-style meal. Serve it with the biggest, juiciest tomatoes you can find, and top your dessert with whatever fresh berries are available.

Menu for 4

- **Malibu Burgers**
- **Corn Chips**
- **Herbed Tomatoes**
- **Berry Cake**

SHOPPING LIST

- ☐ 1 bunch fresh basil or dried basil
- ☐ 1 bunch radishes
- ☐ 4 large ripe tomatoes
- ☐ 1 head Bibb or Boston lettuce
- ☐ 1 small package alfalfa sprouts
- ☐ 1 ripe avocado
- ☐ 1 pint fresh blueberries, strawberries, blackberries or raspberries
- ☐ 1 bunch fresh basil or dried basil
- ☐ 1 small package whole wheat pita breads
- ☐ 1 package corn chips
- ☐ 1 small pound cake
- ☐ 1 8-ounce container sour cream
- ☐ 1 pound ground beef

Have on Hand

- ☐ Salt
- ☐ Sugar
- ☐ 1 lemon or lemon juice
- ☐ Red pepper sauce
- ☐ Vanilla extract

SCHEDULE

1. Mix sour cream topping for dessert; refrigerate.
2. Prepare Herbed Tomatoes.
3. Make avocado topping and cook Malibu Burgers.
4. Assemble Berry Cake.

Malibu Burgers

1 pound ground beef
   Salt
⅔ cup mashed ripe avocado
4 radishes, sliced
1 tablespoon lemon juice
⅛ teaspoon red pepper sauce
4 whole wheat pita breads
½ cup alfalfa sprouts

Shape beef into 4 patties. Sprinkle an even layer of salt over bottom of large heavy skillet. Heat skillet until very hot. Lower heat to medium, add patties and brown well on one side, about 5 minutes. Turn and cook 3 minutes more for medium rare to medium.

In small bowl combine mashed avocado, sliced radishes, ¼ teaspoon salt, lemon juice and red pepper sauce. Split pitas to open pockets. Fill each pita with 1 burger, 3 tablespoons avocado mixture and 2 tablespoons alfalfa sprouts.

Herbed Tomatoes

4 large ripe tomatoes
   Boston or Bibb lettuce
   leaves
1 tablespoon finely minced
   fresh basil or 1½ tea-
   spoons dried basil
1½ teaspoons sugar

Cut tomatoes into ½-inch slices. Arrange on lettuce leaves and sprinkle with basil and sugar.

Berry Cake

1 cup sour cream
2 teaspoons sugar
½ teaspoon vanilla extract
1 cup blueberries, strawberries, blackberries or
   raspberries
4 slices pound cake

In small bowl combine sour cream, sugar and vanilla. Place 1 slice pound cake on each of 4 serving plates. Spoon berries over cake and top with sour cream mixture.

THAWING FROZEN GROUND BEEF

- *Thaw in refrigerator; meat must be kept cold to prevent growth of bacteria.*
- *To thaw quickly, place frozen meat in watertight wrapper and submerge in cold water or in a closed double paper bag at room temperature; cook it as soon as it has thawed.*
- *Thaw beef in microwave oven if you have one.*

Crab Cakes

A FIFTEEN-MINUTE MEAL FOR A SUMMER DAY

Toss together this easy meal on one of those perfect days when it's just too nice to stay inside and cook. Serve it on the porch or patio where you can enjoy the breeze. You can substitute deli salad next time you serve this quickie.

Menu for 4

- **Crab Cakes**
- **Green Pepper Cole Slaw**

Potato Sticks
- **Piña Colada Sundaes**

SHOPPING LIST

- ☐ 1   pound crabmeat
- ☐ 1   green pepper
- ☐ 1   pound carrots
- ☐ 1   small onion
- ☐ 1   bunch parsley
- ☐ 1   7-ounce can potato sticks
- ☐ 1   8¼-ounce can crushed pineapple in syrup
- ☐ 1   small can or package shredded coconut
- ☐ 1   pound cole slaw

Have on Hand
- ☐   Salt
- ☐   Pepper
- ☐   Celery salt
- ☐   Eggs
- ☐   Butter or margarine
- ☐   Mayonnaise
- ☐   Dijon mustard
- ☐   Bread crumbs
- ☐   Raisins
- ☐   Dark rum

SCHEDULE

1. Toast coconut.
2. Toss Green Pepper Cole Slaw; refrigerate.
3. Prepare Crab Cakes.
4. Prepare Piña Colada Sundaes.

Crab Cakes

1   pound crabmeat
1   egg
2   tablespoons mayonnaise
1   tablespoon Dijon mustard
1/2 teaspoon salt
1/4 teaspoon pepper
1/4 teaspoon celery salt
2   tablespoons chopped fresh
       parsley
1/2 cup dried bread crumbs
1   tablespoon butter or
       margarine

In medium bowl combine crabmeat with remaining ingredients except bread crumbs and butter or margarine. Shape into 4 patties and coat with bread crumbs. In large skillet melt butter or margarine; add crab cakes and brown on both sides.

Green Pepper Cole Slaw

1   pound deli cole slaw
1/3 cup chopped green pepper
3   tablespoons minced onion
1/2 cup raisins
1/2 cup grated carrot

In large bowl toss together all ingredients. Refrigerate until serving time.

Piña Colada Sundaes

1/3 cup shredded coconut
1   can (8¼ oz.) crushed pine-
       apple in syrup, drained
4   tablespoons dark rum
1   pint vanilla or coconut ice
       cream

Preheat oven to 350° F. Spread coconut on shallow pan and toast until lightly browned, 3 to 5 minutes, shaking pan once. Remove and set aside. Combine pineapple and rum. Place 1 scoop ice cream in each of 4 dessert dishes. Top with pineapple sauce and sprinkle with toasted coconut.

ANOTHER PIÑA COLADA DESSERT

Into each of 4 parfait glasses spoon 2 rounded tablespoons pineapple-coconut or vanilla yogurt. Top with 2 tablespoons crushed coconut macaroons, then 3 tablespoons drained crushed pineapple. Repeat layers.

Warm Weather Tips

Another Crabmeat Appetizer

Crab Dip: Stir together ½ pound crabmeat, ½ cup sour cream, 1 tablespoon minced onion and 1 tablespoon lemon juice; serve with green pepper rings and carrot sticks.

More Celery Stuffers

Deviled Ham Stalks: Combine 2 cans (4½ oz. each) deviled ham, 1½ teaspoons grated onion, 1½ teaspoons mustard, 2 table-spoons mayonnaise and a dash of red pepper sauce; fill celery stalks and top with chopped pimiento or olives.

Three-Cheese Celery: Stir together 1 cup (¼ lb.) shredded Ched-dar cheese, ½ cup (2 oz.) crumbled blue cheese and 1½ ounces cream cheese (half of a 3-oz. package). Pack into celery stalks; sprinkle with paprika.

Lemon Tips

Easy Lemonade with Old-Time Goodness: Start with Lemon Syrup. Combine 1 cup sugar, 1½ cups warm water and 1 tablespoon grated lemon peel. Stir until sugar is dissolved. Add 1½ cups lemon juice (from 8-10 lemons), cover and refrigerate. When you're ready to serve frosty glasses of homemade lemonade, for each pour ⅓ cup of the Lemon Syrup into a 10-ounce glass. Add ⅔ cup cold water, mineral water or club soda. Stir. Fill up with ice cubes. To prepare a pitcher of frosty refreshment, add 3 cups Lemon Syrup and 6 cups liquid. Stir well. Add ice cubes. Makes nine 8-ounce servings.

Lemonade Twists: For flavor changes, instead of water, charge with fizzy ginger ale, quinine water, iced tea, cranberry juice, a dry white or rosé wine. For garnishes, stick in a sprig of fresh mint, top with a lemon cartwheel, or for a delicate taste, try the old-fashioned trick of dunking strips of cucumber rind. For added interest, shake in a few drops of almond extract or grenadine, a shot of rum, a scoop of fruit sherbet. Or add a delightful surprise—freeze a fresh strawberry in every ice cube.

To liven up Iced Tea in an instant: Make lemonade ice cubes when you make lemonade. Pop them into the glasses, and serve.

Easy Ice Cream Sandwiches

Soften your favorite flavor ice cream slightly and scoop onto one 3-inch cookie (oatmeal, chocolate, sugar, ginger, etc.). Top with a second cookie and roll in choice of toppings (mini chocolate chips, sprinkles, colored sugars). Freeze until ready to serve.

Barbecue Tip

Beef: Remember to trim and score fat. For medium-rare, plan on 7 minutes per side for 1-inch thick strip steak; 8-9 minutes per side for 1¼-inch T-bone, club, sirloin or porterhouse steak; 10-15 minutes on each side for 2-inch London Broil. Minus 2 minutes per side for rare. Test steaks for doneness with the quick finger-test. After the first (and only) turning, touch with your fingertip. If steak feels soft, it's rare. A little firmer, medium. Firm—it's well done.

Tuna Vegetable Platter, page 36

Tuna Vegetable Platter

LAZY-DAY SUPPER WITH A MINTY DESSERT

Here's a cool but nourishing dinner you can prepare just before serving or early in the day. The tuna vegetable platter gets its tang from a smooth mustard-flavored yogurt dressing that you'll want to serve with other salads as well.

Menu for 4

- **Tuna Vegetable Platter**
- **Crusty Bread with Lemon Pepper Butter**
- **Frosted Grasshoppers**

SHOPPING LIST

- ☐ 1   13-ounce can tuna
- ☐ 1   bunch broccoli
- ☐ 2   tomatoes
- ☐ 1   bunch fresh mint
- ☐ 1   8-ounce can red kidney beans
- ☐ 1   14-ounce can artichoke hearts
- ☐ 1   10-ounce package frozen asparagus spears
- ☐ 1   loaf French bread
- ☐ 1   8-ounce container plain yogurt
- ☐ 1   pint vanilla ice cream
- ☐   Green creme de menthe
- ☐   White creme de cacao

Have on Hand

- ☐   Butter or margarine
- ☐   Garlic
- ☐   Mayonnaise
- ☐   Dijon mustard
- ☐   Lemon pepper seasoning

SCHEDULE

1. Prepare Lemon Pepper Butter.
2. Parboil broccoli and assemble Tuna Vegetable Platter.
3. Mix Frosted Grasshoppers.

Tuna Vegetable Platter

½ bunch broccoli
¾ cup mayonnaise
¼ cup plain yogurt
1 small garlic clove, halved
1 tablespoon Dijon mustard
1 cup canned red kidney beans, drained and rinsed
1 can (14 oz.) artichoke hearts, drained
1 package (10 oz.) frozen asparagus spears, thawed
2 tomatoes, cut into wedges
1 can (13 oz.) tuna, drained

Cut off broccoli florets and plunge into salted boiling water; cook 4 minutes. (Save stems and remaining broccoli for another meal.) Drain and plunge into cold water to cool. Drain again. In small bowl combine mayonnaise, yogurt, garlic and mustard. Arrange broccoli, remaining vegetables and tuna on serving platter. Spoon half the mayonnaise-mustard dressing over top; serve remainder in small bowl.

Crusty Bread with Lemon Pepper Butter

½ cup softened butter or margarine

½ teaspoon lemon pepper seasoning
1 loaf French bread, heated

In small bowl combine butter or margarine and lemon pepper. Pack into small serving bowl. Serve with French bread.

Frosted Grasshoppers

¼ cup green creme de menthe
¼ cup white creme de cacao
1 pint vanilla ice cream
  Fresh mint sprigs

Combine creme de menthe and creme de cacao in blender container; add ice cream. Cover and whirl just until blended. Pour into stemmed glasses. Garnish with mint.

ADD A REFRESHING TOUCH OF MINT

- *Iced tea and buttered carrots are natural partners for mint, but you can also:*
- *fill melon halves with vanilla ice cream, drizzle orange-flavored liqueur over them and top with mint sprigs*
- *add chopped mint leaves to hot peas*
- *add chopped mint leaves to cold, cooked rice tossed with lemon vinaigrette.*

Tuna Avocado Salad, page 40

Sundae with Quick Chocolate Sauce, page 42

Turkey Cobb Salad, page 44

Burrito Burgers, page 46 ▶

Tuna-Avocado Salad

MAIN-DISH SALAD WITH A BLENDER SOUP

Serve this dill-flavored tomato soup cold on scorching summer days; heat it when there's a nip of fall in the air. Dress up the meal by serving the salad on a bed of shredded lettuce garnished with lemon wedges.

Menu for 4

- **Dilled Tomato Soup**
- **Pita Snacks**
- **Tuna-Avocado Salad Lemon-Coconut Layer Cake**

SHOPPING LIST

- ☐ 1 13-ounce can tuna
- ☐ 1 bunch green onions
- ☐ 1 bunch fresh dill (optional)
- ☐ 1 bunch celery
- ☐ 1 head lettuce
- ☐ 2 avocados
- ☐ 1 8-ounce container sour cream
- ☐ 4 pita breads
- ☐ 2 14½-ounce cans stewed tomatoes
- ☐ 1 bottle Russian dressing
- ☐ 1 lemon-coconut layer cake

Have on Hand
- ☐   Butter or margarine

- ☐ 1 lemon or lemon juice
- ☐   Horseradish
- ☐   Dillweed
- ☐   Red pepper sauce
- ☐   Chicken bouillon granules
- ☐   Bacon

SCHEDULE

1. Blend Dilled Tomato Soup; refrigerate.
2. Prepare Pita Snacks and set aside.
3. Prepare Tuna Avocado Salad.
4. Heat Pita Snacks.

Dilled Tomato Soup

2 cans (14 ½ oz. each)
    stewed tomatoes
¾ cup hot water
1 teaspoon chicken bouillon
    granules or 1 bouillon
    cube
1½ teaspoons lemon juice
2 tablespoons sour cream
1 teaspoon horseradish
¼ teaspoon dillweed
3 drops red pepper sauce
    Extra sour cream for
        garnish (optional)
    Fresh dill sprigs for gar-
        nish (optional)

In blender combine stewed tomatoes and juice, hot water, bouillon granules and lemon juice. Cover and blend until smooth. Add sour cream, horseradish, dillweed and red pepper sauce; cover and blend again until smooth. Pour into large bowl; refrigerate until serving time. Garnish with sour cream and a sprig of fresh dill, if you wish. (Soup can be heated and served hot.)

Pita Snacks

4 pita breads
4 tablespoons butter or
    margarine, softened
½ teaspoon dillweed

Preheat broiler or toaster oven. Split pita breads. In small bowl combine butter or margarine and dillweed; blend well. Spread dill butter on pita; cut each half into 4 wedges. Broil until crisp.

Tuna-Avocado Salad

1 can (13 oz.) tuna, drained
¼ cup sliced green onions
¼ cup chopped celery
½ cup bottled Russian
    dressing
1 teaspoon lemon juice
2 avocados
    Shredded lettuce
3 slices bacon, cooked and
    crumbled

In large bowl combine tuna, green onions, celery, Russian dressing and lemon juice; toss. Cut avocados in half; remove pits. Place on shredded lettuce on serving platter. Fill each avocado half with tuna salad; top with crumbled bacon.

TUNA TIP

Tuna Appetizers: *To make these festive party snacks, cut tops off cherry tomatoes and scoop out seeds. Then stuff each tomato with tuna salad and garnish with fresh dill sprigs.*

Tuna Tacos

AVOCADO AND TUNA SANDWICHES

Here is a surprisingly delicious combination of flavors and textures, from creamy avocado to crisp, cool lettuce to peppery taco sauce. Serve with fresh green beans and a chocolate dessert for a new taste experience.

Menu for 4

- **Tuna Tacos**
- **Sauteed Green Beans**
  Carrot Sticks

- **Vanilla Ice Cream with Quick Chocolate Sauce**

SHOPPING LIST

- ☐ 1 6½- or 7-ounce can tuna
- ☐ 1 head iceberg lettuce
- ☐ 1 small onion
- ☐ 1 bunch green onions
- ☐ 1 pound green beans
- ☐ 1 bunch carrots
- ☐ 1 large tomato
- ☐ 1 ripe avocado
- ☐ 1 16-ounce can chocolate-flavored syrup
- ☐ 2 4-ounce cans taco sauce
- ☐ 1 4-ounce can chopped pimientos
- ☐ 1 package taco shells
- ☐ 1 4-ounce package shredded Cheddar cheese

- ☐ 1 pint vanilla ice cream

Have on Hand
- ☐ Salt
- ☐ Pepper
- ☐ Garlic salt
- ☐ Butter or margarine
- ☐ unsweetened chocolate

SCHEDULE

1. Prepare carrot sticks.
2. Prepare Quick Chocolate Sauce.
3. Prepare Sauteed Green Beans.
4. Prepare Tuna Tacos.

Tuna Tacos

1   can (6 ½ or 7 oz.) *tuna,*
      drained and flaked
2   cans (4 oz. each) *taco*
      sauce
½   teaspoon *garlic salt*
½   cup *shredded iceberg*
      lettuce
4   packaged *taco shells,*
      heated
1   cup (4 oz.) *shredded*
      Cheddar cheese
1   large *tomato, chopped*
1   ripe *avocado, peeled,*
      pitted and chopped
½   cup *chopped green onions*

In small bowl combine tuna, taco sauce and garlic salt. Place 2 tablespoons lettuce in each taco shell; spoon in about ⅓ cup tuna mixture. Sprinkle each with cheese, tomato, avocado and green onions.

Sauteed Green Beans

1   pound *fresh whole green*
      beans, trimmed
2   tablespoons *butter or*
      margarine
1   tablespoon *minced onion*
2   tablespoons *chopped*
      pimiento

In large saucepan cook beans in salted water to cover 4 to 5 minutes just until tender; drain. In large skillet heat butter or margarine until bubbly but not brown.

Add onion and cook until translucent; add beans and saute 2 to 3 minutes. Transfer to serving dish and toss with chopped pimiento.

Vanilla Ice Cream with Quick Chocolate Sauce

1   can (16 oz.) *chocolate-*
      flavored syrup
1   square (1 oz.) *unsweetened*
      chocolate
1   tablespoon *butter or*
      margarine
1   pint *vanilla ice cream*

In small saucepan heat syrup, chocolate square and butter or margarine until melted and smooth. Set aside.

Place 1 scoop vanilla ice cream in each of 4 dessert dishes and top with chocolate sauce. Refrigerate remaining sauce.

Note: Sauce can be warmed up and served as hot fudge or refrigerated and served cold over ice cream, cake or fruit. Cover and refrigerate up to 2 weeks.

TACO TIPS

To heat packaged taco shells: Preheat oven to 350° F. Put shells on cookie sheet or hang them over bars of oven shelf. Heat 10 minutes, turning once if on cookie sheet. In microwave: Crisp taco shells 30 seconds.

Turkey Cobb Salad

TURKEY AND FRESH VEGETABLES

Cobb salad is usually made with chicken, but you can make this equally good version with turkey from the delicatessen. The secret here, as with many main-dish salads, is to create a striking arrangement of the ingredients when you present the dish.

Menu for 4

- **Peach Cantaloupe Soup**
- **Turkey Cobb Salad**

Sesame Rolls
Pink Peppermint Ice Cream and Cookies

SHOPPING LIST

- ☐ 1 pound cooked turkey breast
- ☐ ½ pound bacon
- ☐ 1 head iceberg lettuce
- ☐ 2 medium tomatoes
- ☐ 1 bunch green onions
- ☐ 1 medium-ripe cantaloupe
- ☐ 2 medium-ripe peaches
- ☐ 1 package sesame rolls
- ☐ 1 box cookies
- ☐ 1 pint buttermilk
- ☐ 2 ounces blue cheese
- ☐ 1 quart pink peppermint ice cream

Have on Hand

- ☐ Salt

- ☐ Pepper
- ☐ Dry mustard
- ☐ Sugar
- ☐ Garlic
- ☐ Olive oil
- ☐ Salad oil
- ☐ Red wine vinegar
- ☐ Orange juice
- ☐ Dry white wine

SCHEDULE

1. Prepare Peach Cantaloupe Soup; refrigerate.
2. Prepare Cobb Salad.

Peach Cantaloupe Soup

1   medium-ripe cantaloupe, seeded, scooped from rind and cut into chunks
1   medium-ripe peach, peeled, pitted and cut into chunks
1/3   cup dry white wine
1/3   cup orange juice
1   tablespoon sugar
1¼   cups buttermilk
1   fresh peach, peeled, pitted and sliced, for garnish

In food processor or blender, combine cantaloupe, peach, wine, orange juice and sugar; process or blend until almost smooth. Add buttermilk; process until well blended. Refrigerate until serving time. Serve in chilled bowls and garnish with sliced peaches.

Turkey Cobb Salad

½   teaspoon salt
⅛   teaspoon pepper
¼   teaspoon dry mustard
3   tablespoons red wine vinegar
1   garlic clove, crushed
1/3   cup olive oil
3   tablespoons salad oil
1   medium head iceberg lettuce, shredded
3   green onions, cut into 2-inch pieces
2   medium tomatoes, seeded and chopped
1   pound cooked turkey breast, cut into chunks
2   ounces blue cheese, crumbled
4   slices bacon, cooked and crumbled

In jar with tight-fitting lid combine salt, pepper, mustard, vinegar, garlic and oils. Shake well. Place lettuce in salad bowl or on platter. Arrange onions, tomatoes, chunks of turkey, cheese and bacon on lettuce. Sprinkle dressing over salad at serving time.

ICE CREAM TIPS

• *Keep ice cream in containers with tight lids to avoid loss of moisture during time in the freezer.*
• *To avoid crystallization after package has been opened, cover surface of ice cream with plastic wrap before replacing lid.*
• *Ice cream is best stored at 10 to 0 degrees F. At these temperatures it will remain firm but pliable. Before serving allow to stand in refrigerator 20 minutes for a ½ gallon, 5 minutes for a pint.*

Burrito Burgers in Tortillas

SOUTH-OF-THE-BORDER BARBECUE

These spicy burgers come with a selection of refried beans, vegetables and salsa—all piled into warm tortillas. The tasty and unusual salad is flavored the Mexican way with cilantro and chili powder. Add peaches marinated in wine for a summery end to a perfect meal.

Menu for 4

- **Burrito Burgers in Tortillas**
- **Cilantro Cucumber Salad**
- **Sangria Peaches**

SHOPPING LIST

- ☐ 2 bunches green onions
- ☐ 2 medium cucumbers
- ☐ 1 head iceberg lettuce
- ☐ 3 large ripe peaches or 1 20-ounce bag frozen sliced peaches
- ☐ 1 lime or bottled lime juice
- ☐ 1 bunch fresh cilantro or parsley
- ☐ 1 package flour tortillas
- ☐ 1 15-ounce can refried beans
- ☐ 1 small bottle salsa
- ☐ 1 pound ground beef

Have on Hand
- ☐ Salt

- ☐ Sugar
- ☐ Cumin
- ☐ Chili powder
- ☐ Dried coriander
- ☐ Cinnamon sticks
- ☐ Dry white wine

SCHEDULE

1. Prepare Sangria Peaches; chill.
2. Prepare Cilantro Cucumber Salad; chill.
3. Prepare Burrito Burgers.

Burrito Burgers

1   cup chopped green onions,
      divided
1   cup bottled salsa, divided
1/4 teaspoon cumin
      Dash salt
1   pound ground beef
      Flour tortillas, warmed
1   can (15 oz.) refried beans
      Shredded lettuce

Prepare grill or preheat broiler. In medium bowl combine 2 tablespoons green onions, 2 tablespoons salsa, cumin and salt with ground beef. Mix lightly and shape into 4 oval patties. Grill or broil 4 to 6 inches from heat 3 minutes on each side. Place burgers on warm tortillas; top with refried beans, green onions, lettuce and salsa. Fold one side of tortilla up and the two adjacent sides inward; fold fourth side over to enclose burger.

Cilantro Cucumber Salad

2   medium cucumbers
2   tablespoons lime juice
1   teaspoon chili powder
1/4 teaspoon salt
1   tablespoon chopped cilantro
      or parsley with 1/4
      teaspoon dried coriander

Peel cucumbers, quarter lengthwise and cut into 1-inch pieces. Place in bowl. Sprinkle with lime juice, chili powder and salt; toss. Add fresh cilantro or parsley and dried coriander and toss again. Chill until serving time.

Sangria Peaches

1 1/2 cups dry white wine
1/3   cup sugar
1   cinnamon stick, broken
2 1/2 cups fresh or frozen sliced
       peaches

In medium saucepan combine wine and sugar. Add cinnamon stick and bring to a boil. Cook 1 minute, stirring until sugar dissolves. Add peaches; return to a boil and cook 2 minutes. Pour into large bowl and place in freezer until serving time. Remove cinnamon stick before serving. (Reserve any leftover syrup to use as base for sangria.)

SPEEDY SALSA

To make this Mexican condiment, place in blender: 2 large ripe tomatoes, 2 chopped canned chilies, 1 small chopped onion, 1 tablespoon chopped cilantro (fresh coriander) and 1/4 teaspoon salt. Blend until combined but still somewhat chunky.

Pita Pocket Burgers, page 50

Salade Nicoise, page 52

Pocket Burgers

ALFRESCO DINING, MEDITERRANEAN STYLE

Tucked inside tasty pita breads, these lightly spiced beef patties are topped with a smooth cucumber-yogurt sauce. The carrot salad is extra-special with fresh mint, but dried mint teamed with parsley makes a viable substitute. Team them up with a dessert of fresh seasonal fruit.

Menu for 4

- **Pocket Burgers**
- **Carrot-Mint Salad**

- **Potato Chips**
- **Glazed Fresh Fruit**

SHOPPING LIST

- ☐ 4   pita breads
- ☐ 1   small cucumber
- ☐ 1   large tomato
- ☐ 1   small onion
- ☐ 1   head lettuce
- ☐ 1   pint fresh blueberries
- ☐ 1   pound nectarines
- ☐ 2   lemons or 1 lemon and lemon juice
- ☐ 1   bunch fresh mint (or dried mint and fresh parsley)
- ☐ 1   8-ounce container plain yogurt
- ☐ 1   20-ounce bag frozen carrots
- ☐ 1½   pounds ground beef

Have on Hand

- ☐   Salt
- ☐   Pepper
- ☐   Garlic powder
- ☐   Sugar
- ☐   Salad oil
- ☐   Cumin
- ☐   Orange marmalade

SCHEDULE

1. Prepare Carrot-Mint Salad.
2. Prepare Glazed Fresh Fruit.
3. Prepare Pocket Burgers.

Pocket Burgers

1½	*pounds ground beef*
¾	*teaspoon salt, divided*
½	*teaspoon garlic powder,*
	divided
¼	*teaspoon ground cumin*
½	*cup plain yogurt*
⅓	*cup seeded chopped*
	cucumber
1	*small onion, diced*
4	*pita breads*
4	*thick slices tomato*

Place ground beef in large bowl and sprinkle with ½ teaspoon salt, ¼ teaspoon garlic powder and cumin. Mix lightly and shape into 4 patties. Broil or grill 3 minutes on each side, turning once.

Meanwhile, in medium bowl combine yogurt, cucumber, onion, ¼ teaspoon salt and ¼ teaspoon garlic powder. Slit one side of each pita to open pocket. Tuck in 1 burger and 1 tomato slice; top with cucumber sauce.

Carrot-Mint Salad

3	*cups frozen sliced carrots*
3	*tablespoons chopped fresh*
	mint or 1 teaspoon dried
	mint and 3 tablespoons
	chopped parsley
¼	*cup salad oil*
3	*tablespoons sugar*
3	*tablespoons lemon juice*
⅛	*teaspoon salt*
	Dash pepper
	Lettuce leaves

Thaw carrots in colander under cold running water; drain. Combine in medium bowl with chopped mint. In jar with tight-fitting lid combine salad oil, lemon juice, sugar, salt and pepper; cover and shake. Pour over minted carrots and toss. Arrange on lettuce leaves in salad bowl or on individual serving plates.

Glazed Fresh Fruit

2	*cups blueberries*
1	*pound nectarines, sliced*
¼	*cup orange marmalade*
2	*tablespoons lemon juice*
1	*teaspoon grated lemon peel*

In large bowl combine blueberries and nectarines. In small saucepan heat marmalade, lemon juice and peel, stirring constantly until mixture begins to boil. Pour over fruit and toss until well coated.

BUYING GROUND BEEF

Ground chuck, which has 15 to 25 percent fat, makes a juicy and flavorful burger. Ground round is fine for other beef dishes, but it does make a less juicy burger because it has only 11 percent fat. Make sure package is not torn and feels cold. Purchase ground beef just before you leave the store; get it home quickly and refrigerate or freeze immediately.

Salade Niçoise

A FRENCH SALAD CLASSIC

Here is an opportunity to serve a meal that is delicious, quick and beautiful. Instead of cooking, you can spend your time creating a perfect presentation. Check the Tips section for ways to vary this meal.

Menu for 4

- **Clubhouse Lemonade**
- **Salade Niçoise**

- **French-Style Hard Rolls**
- **Blueberry Tarts**

SHOPPING LIST

- ☐ 1   13-ounce can tuna
- ☐ 2   large or 4 small tomatoes
- ☐ 1   head lettuce
- ☐ 1   red onion
- ☐ 1   pint fresh blueberries
- ☐ 7   lemons
- ☐ 4   prepared tart shells
- ☐ 1   16-ounce can small whole white potatoes
- ☐ 1   16-ounce can whole green beans
- ☐ 1   small can ripe olives
- ☐ 1   small can anchovy fillets
- ☐ 1   small can chopped walnuts
- ☐ 4   French-style hard rolls

- ☐ ½   pint heavy or whipping cream

Have on Hand
- ☐   Sugar
- ☐   Black or red currant jelly
- ☐   Dijon mustard
- ☐   Bottled Italian salad dressing

SCHEDULE

1. Prepare Blueberry Tarts; whip cream, chop walnuts. Refrigerate separately.
2. Mix Clubhouse Lemonade.
3. Prepare Salade Niçoise.

Clubhouse Lemonade

1 cup fresh lemon juice
3/4 cup sugar, or to taste
4 cups cold water
1 lemon, thinly sliced
    Ice cubes

In large pitcher combine lemon juice and sugar. Stir to dissolve sugar. Add remaining ingredients. Blend well.

Salade Niçoise

3/4   cup bottled Italian salad dressing
1½ teaspoons Dijon mustard
    Lettuce leaves
1   can (13 oz.) tuna, drained
2   large or 4 small tomatoes, cut into wedges
1   can (16 oz.) whole white potatoes, drained and quartered
1   can (16 oz.) whole green beans, drained
12 ripe olives
8   anchovy fillets
1   red onion, sliced and separated into rings

In 1-cup measure combine salad dressing with mustard. Line a large platter or 4 individual dinner plates with lettuce leaves. Arrange tuna, tomato wedges, potatoes and green beans on lettuce. Garnish with olives, anchovy fillets and onion rings. Sprinkle with dressing.

Blueberry Tarts

1 pint fresh blueberries
4 prepared tart shells
1 tablespoon black or red currant jelly
½ cup whipped cream
¼ cup chopped walnuts

Wash and drain blueberries. Divide evenly among tart shells. In small saucepan melt currant jelly over very low heat. With pastry brush glaze berries with melted jelly. Garnish with whipped cream and sprinkle with chopped walnuts.

SALADE NIÇOISE TIPS

- *In place of canned potatoes, use prepared potato salad from the deli.*
- *Use fresh cooked green beans; cool quickly in ice water and drain well.*
- *Early in the day prepare hard-cooked eggs. Refrigerate; cut into wedges and use as garnish.*
- *Serve the salad with a chilled dry rosé wine.*

Classic Hero, page 56 ◆   ◆ *Sausage and Pepper Hero,*
page 58

Classic Heroes

EASY SUPPER WITH A COOL DESSERT

On those evenings when it's just too hot to cook, serve a popular favorite—the ham, salami and cheese hero. Add potato salad and raw vegetables to make this meal an indoor picnic. Then surprise your family with a cool and colorful dessert.

Menu for 4

- **Classic Heroes**
  German
     Potato Salad
- **Carrot Sticks**
     with Creamy
     Avocado Dip
        • **Summer Rainbow**

SHOPPING LIST

- ☐ ¼ pound thinly sliced salami
- ☐ ½ pound sliced ham
- ☐ 2 medium tomatoes
- ☐ 2 small onions
- ☐ 1 pound carrots
- ☐ 1 head iceberg lettuce
- ☐ 1 ripe avocado
- ☐ 4 6- to 8-inch hero rolls
- ☐ ½ pound sliced provolone cheese
- ☐ 1 pound deli German potato salad
- ☐ 1 8-ounce container plain yogurt
- ☐ ½ pint each orange, lime and raspberry or strawberry sherbet

- ☐ 1 small jar raspberry topping (Melba sauce)

Have on Hand
- ☐ Salt
- ☐ White pepper
- ☐ Bottled Italian dressing

SCHEDULE

1. Clean carrots and cut into sticks; prepare Creamy Avocado Dip.
2. Assemble Classic Heroes.
3. Prepare Summer Rainbow.

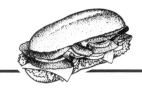

Classic Heroes

¼ *pound thinly sliced salami*
½ *pound sliced provolone*
  cheese
½ *pound sliced ham*
4 *hero rolls (6-8 in.), split*
2 *medium tomatoes, sliced*
1 *small onion, thinly sliced*
2 *cups shredded iceberg*
  lettuce
  Bottled Italian dressing

Layer salami, cheese and ham on bottom halves of rolls; top with tomato slices, onion slices and lettuce. Sprinkle dressing over lettuce. Replace tops of rolls.

Summer Rainbow

½ *pint orange sherbet*
½ *pint lime sherbet*
½ *pint raspberry or*
  strawberry sherbet
  Bottled raspberry topping
  (Melba sauce)

Fill 4 parfait glasses with layers of the three sherbets. Top with raspberry sauce.

Creamy Avocado Dip

1 *ripe avocado, peeled and*
  pitted
1 *container (8 oz.) plain*
  yogurt
2 *tablespoons minced onion*
¼ *teaspoon salt*
⅛ *teaspoon white pepper*
  Carrot sticks

In medium bowl mash avocado. Add yogurt, onion, salt and white pepper. Stir until blended. Serve with carrot sticks.

SANDWICH TIPS

• Deli Heroes: *Slice French bread horizontally and pile on Swiss cheese, bologna, olive loaf, tomato and lettuce; sprinkle with salad dressing.*
• Juniors: *Spread peanut butter on cracked wheat bread slices; add apple rings, American cheese and lettuce; top with second bread slices.*
• Whole Wheat Roll-Ups: *Spread whole wheat bread slices with guacamole, then sprinkle with bean sprouts or alfalfa sprouts; roll up jelly-roll fashion. Secure with toothpicks.*

Sausage and Pepper Heroes

SATISFYING SANDWICH SUPPER

The thick, juicy and highly spiced Sausage and Pepper Hero is a popular feature of the summer festivals in large Italian neighborhoods. Mix some hot sausage in with the sweet if you wish, tuck some red peppers among the green.

═══ Menu for 4 ═══

- **Sausage and Pepper Heroes**
- **Italian Salad with Gorgonzola Cheese**
- **Peach Pound Cake**

SHOPPING LIST

- ☐ 1 pound sweet Italian sausage
- ☐ 1½ pounds peppers, green, red or mixed
- ☐ 3 medium onions
- ☐ 2 heads Boston or Bibb lettuce
- ☐ 4 peaches
- ☐ 4 6- to 8-inch hero rolls
- ☐ 1 small pound cake
- ☐ 4 ounces Gorgonzola cheese
- ☐ 1 8-ounce container sour cream

Have on Hand

- ☐ Salt
- ☐ Pepper
- ☐ Oregano
- ☐ Sugar
- ☐ Garlic
- ☐ Olive oil
- ☐ Red wine vinegar
- ☐ 1 lemon or lemon juice

SCHEDULE

1. Prepare sausage and peppers.
2. Prepare Italian Salad with Gorgonzola Cheese.
3. Assemble Sausage and Pepper Heroes.
4. Prepare Peach Pound Cake.

Sausage and Pepper Heroes

1	tablespoon olive oil
1	pound sweet Italian sausage
¼	cup water
1½	pounds peppers, green, red or mixed, cut into chunks
3	medium onions, sliced
3	garlic cloves, finely chopped
½	teaspoon oregano
4	hero rolls (6-8 in.), split and heated

In large, heavy skillet heat oil over medium-high heat. Add sausage and brown well. Pour in water and cook over medium heat until cooked through, about 10 minutes. Remove and drain sausage but do not turn off heat. Slice ½ inch thick.

When water has evaporated from skillet, add sausage, peppers, onions, garlic and oregano. Cook, stirring often, 10 to 15 minutes. Spoon into hero rolls.

Italian Salad with Gorgonzola Cheese

3	tablespoons olive oil
1½	teaspoons red wine vinegar
1½	teaspoons lemon juice
⅛	teaspoon salt
	Dash pepper
5	cups Boston or Bibb lettuce, torn into bite-sized pieces
4	ounces Gorgonzola cheese, crumbled

In small jar with tight-fitting lid, combine oil, vinegar, lemon juice, salt and pepper; cover and shake well. In salad bowl combine lettuce and crumbled cheese. Sprinkle with dressing and toss well.

Peach Pound Cake

1	cup sour cream
2	tablespoons sugar
1	cup sliced peaches
4	slices pound cake

In small bowl combine sour cream and sugar. Arrange ¼ cup sliced peaches on each slice of pound cake. Top with sweetened sour cream.

QUICK ITALIAN SANDWICHES FOR SUMMER MEALS

- Salami Favorites: *Slit open and butter 4 pita breads. Stuff each with ¼ cup shredded lettuce, ¼ cup shredded mozzarella cheese, ¼ cup cubed salami and 2 tablespoons chopped marinated mushrooms.*
- Pizza-Style Grilled Cheese: *Place thin slices of mozzarella cheese on 4 slices white or brown bread. Top with 1 tablespoon pizza sauce and 1 tablespoon chopped salami or pepperoni; grill in skillet, broiler or toaster oven.*

Muffuletta with Olive Salad

SANDWICH MEAL IN AN ITALIAN BREAD SHELL

Pair an unusual sandwich with cool and creamy cole slaw for a quick and flavorful no-cook meal. Fresh ripe cherries make a sweet, light dessert, but if you can't find them, substitute another fresh fruit.

═ Menu for 4 ═

- **Muffuletta with**
- **Olive Salad**

- **Cherokee Strip Cole Slaw**
- **Fresh Cherries**

SHOPPING LIST

- ☐ ¼ pound thinly sliced salami
- ☐ ¼ pound sliced ham
- ☐ 1 16-ounce package shredded cabbage
- ☐ 1 pound carrots
- ☐ 1 large red or green pepper
- ☐ Fresh cherries or other seasonal fruit
- ☐ 1 bunch fresh parsley
- ☐ 1 10-ounce jar pimiento-stuffed olives
- ☐ 1 10-ounce can pitted ripe olives
- ☐ 1 8-inch round loaf Italian bread
- ☐ ¼ pound sliced provolone cheese
- ☐ ¼ pound sliced mozzarella cheese
- ☐ ½ pint heavy or whipping cream

Have on Hand

- ☐ Salt
- ☐ Oregano
- ☐ Sugar
- ☐ Garlic
- ☐ Olive oil
- ☐ Cider vinegar
- ☐ Red wine vinegar
- ☐ Capers

SCHEDULE

1. Prepare Olive Salad; set aside.
2. Mix Cherokee Strip Cole Slaw; refrigerate.
3. Prepare Muffuletta.

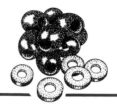

Olive Salad

1½ cups chopped pimiento-
      stuffed olives
½   cup chopped pitted ripe
      olives
1   large red or green
      pepper, chopped
⅓   cup chopped parsley
2   tablespoons drained
      capers
2   tablespoons minced garlic
½   teaspoon oregano
¾   cup olive oil
1   teaspoon red wine
      vinegar

In medium bowl combine all ingredients.
Cover and set aside at room temperature
until serving time.

Muffuletta

1   round (8 in.) loaf Italian
      bread
1   recipe Olive Salad (see
      above)
¼   pound thinly sliced salami
¼   pound sliced provolone
      cheese
¼   pound sliced ham
¼   pound sliced mozzarella
      cheese

With serrated knife, slice about ½ inch
from top of Italian bread loaf. Cut and
scoop out interior, leaving a ½-inch shell.
Drain Olive Salad, reserving dressing.
Brush interior of shell with reserved

dressing; then layer with 1½ cups Olive
Salad, salami, provolone, ham, mozzarella and remaining salad. Replace top of
loaf.

Cherokee Strip
Cole Slaw

1   package (16 oz.) shredded
      cabbage, chopped
½   cup shredded carrots
½   cup heavy or whipping
      cream
⅓   cup sugar
2½ tablespoons cider vinegar
½   teaspoon salt
      Parsley sprigs for garnish

In large bowl combine cabbage and carrots. In small bowl combine cream, sugar,
vinegar and salt; stir until sugar dissolves.
Pour over cabbage and toss until well
coated. Cover and refrigerate until serving time.

COLE SLAW TIPS

*Start with deli or homemade cole
slaw and:*
* *Stir in chopped mandarin oranges,
  chopped peanuts and sliced green
  onions.*
* *Add finely chopped red onion and
  a dash of sesame oil.*

Lobster Salad Rolls

A DELICIOUS MEAL OF FRESH SUMMER FOODS

This menu is certain to become a warm weather favorite. You'll spend only ten minutes in the kitchen, yet will offer some of the summer's greatest dining pleasures—cucumbers, lobster and strawberries.

Menu for 4

- **Chilled Cucumber Dill Soup**
- **Lobster Salad Rolls**
- **Strawberry Shortcake Sundaes**

SHOPPING LIST

- ☐ ¾ pound cooked lobster meat or 2 6-ounce packages frozen langostinos
- ☐ 1 medium onion
- ☐ 3 medium cucumbers
- ☐ 1 bunch celery
- ☐ 1 bunch fresh dill or dillweed
- ☐ 1 bunch parsley (optional)
- ☐ 1 pint fresh strawberries
- ☐ 2 13¾- or 14½-ounce cans chicken broth
- ☐ 1 small package frankfurter rolls
- ☐ 1 package oatmeal cookies
- ☐ 1 8-ounce container plain yogurt
- ☐ 1 quart strawberry ice cream

Have on Hand

- ☐ Salt
- ☐ Pepper
- ☐ Mayonnaise
- ☐ 1 lemon or lemon juice

SCHEDULE

1. Cook and puree cucumbers; place in freezer.
2. Slice strawberries and sprinkle with sugar.
3. Prepare Lobster Salad Rolls.
4. Finish preparing Chilled Cucumber Dill Soup.

Chilled Cucumber Dill Soup ·

3 cups sliced peeled
   cucumbers
2 cups chicken broth
¼ cup finely chopped onion
¼ cup plain yogurt
2 teaspoons fresh dill or ½
   teaspoon dillweed
   Dash pepper
   Fresh dill sprigs or cucumber slices for garnish

In medium saucepan combine cucumbers, broth and onion. Heat to boiling;
reduce heat and cook until cucumbers are
translucent, about 10 minutes. Pour into
blender and puree until smooth. Chill in
freezer until serving time.
   Stir in yogurt, dill and pepper. Garnish
with dill sprigs or cucumber slices.

Lobster Salad Rolls

2 cups diced cooked lobster
   meat or 2 packages
   (6 oz. each) frozen
   langostinos, thawed
   and well drained
¼ cup sliced celery
½ cup mayonnaise, divided
1½ teaspoons fresh lemon
   juice
   Dash pepper
4 frankfurter rolls, split
   Chopped parsley
   (optional)

In large bowl combine lobster, celery, ¼
cup mayonnaise, lemon juice and pepper;
mix well. Spread cut sides of rolls with
remaining mayonnaise. Spoon in filling.
Sprinkle with parsley, if desired.

Strawberry Short-cake Sundaes

1 pint fresh strawberries,
   stemmed and sliced
   Sugar
1 quart strawberry ice cream
4 oatmeal cookies, crumbled

Place berries in bowl and sprinkle with
sugar to taste. Cover and leave at room
temperature until serving time.
   Place 2 scoops strawberry ice cream in
each dessert dish. Spoon strawberries on
top and sprinkle with crumbled cookies.

CELERY STUFFERS

• Brazil Nut Celery: *Let 6 ounces
cream cheese soften at room temperature. Stir in 1 tablespoon
grated onion, ¼ teaspoon salt, a
dash of bottled red pepper sauce
and ½ cup chopped Brazil nuts.
Fill celery stalks with mixture; top
with another ¼ cup Brazil nuts.*
• Confetti Celery: *Chop 1 carrot
and ½ green pepper; stir into ¾
cup cottage cheese. Fill 4 long ribs
of celery. Cut each into pieces
about 3 inches long.*

Warm Weather Tips

More Barbecue Tips

Chicken: A half chicken (1 to 1½ lbs.) makes a generous dinner portion for adults. Chicken stays moist, juicy if you start skin-side down over medium coals. With halves or quarters, it's best to break wing and drumstick joints for more even grilling. Grill breasts over hotter coals—10-12 minutes per side, basting frequently.

Vegetables: Tomato halves get grilled 2-3 minutes on each side (cut side down first). Zucchini, halved and oiled, grills in 5 minutes per side. Eggplant tastes and looks the best unpeeled, cut into slices, oiled and grilled 5 minutes per side. Corn, husked, should be wrapped in foil with butter and salt; grill 20 minutes, turning once. Or, peel back husks, remove silks. Soak corn in cold water for 5 minutes to add steaming power. Grill 20 minutes.

Fish: Always brush fish first with melted butter or oil before placing on grill. Re-baste several times during cooking. A fish steak (¾ inch), such as swordfish, requires 4-6 minutes per side over medium coals. Take extra care—fish is delicate, will flake apart if overhandled. Turn once. There are special wire cages for grilling smaller fish and fillets. If you plan to serve fish often, invest.

Kabobs: Cut meat or fish into 1 to 1½ inch cubes or thread in thin strips. Leave skin on fish to hold together. Parboil whole onions. Go beyond cherry tomqtoes and mushroom caps to the more unusual: parsnips, water chestnuts, Brussels sprouts, corn chunks. Or sweet fruits—cantaloupe, orange slices or sections, pineapple chunks.

General BBQ Tips

Flavor your cooking by using hickory chips. Or throw herbs, garlic cloves or onion skins right on embers. Brushing grill with oil or coating with vegetable cooking spray will help prevent meats from sticking. Season with salt and pepper after grilling— or juices may be drawn out.

Sectioning an Orange

With a sharp knife, remove peel. Slice along dividing membranes on either side of a section, following contours. Life out section. Continue all the way around.

No More Green Yolks

For perfect hard-cooked eggs: Place in saucepan in a single layer; cover with cold water. Bring to just under a boil. Turn off heat; cover and let stand 15 minutes. Drain and immerse in cold water to stop cooking. Refrigerate.

Caesar of the Sea

SALAD WITH A SOUTH SEAS DESSERT

Add a can of tuna to the traditional Caesar Salad to turn it into a quick and cool main dish. Make your own croutons, if you wish, following the directions in the Tips section, or use the packaged variety.

=== **Menu for 4** ===

- **Caesar of the Sea**
  Italian Bread with Butter

- **Polynesian Delight**

SHOPPING LIST

- ☐ 1 13-ounce can tuna
- ☐ 1 medium head romaine lettuce
- ☐ 1 banana
- ☐ 1 mango
- ☐ 1 small package garlic croutons
- ☐ 1 8¼-ounce can crushed pineapple
- ☐ 1 2-ounce can anchovy fillets
- ☐ 1 loaf Italian bread
- ☐ 1 quart pineapple sherbet

Have on Hand
- ☐   Salt
- ☐   Pepper

- ☐   Sugar
- ☐   Butter or margarine
- ☐   Eggs
- ☐   Grated Parmesan cheese
- ☐   Garlic
- ☐   Olive oil
- ☐ 1 lemon or lemon juice

SCHEDULE

1. Toast coconut for dessert.
2. Prepare Caesar of the Sea.
3. Assemble Polynesian Delight.

Caesar of the Sea

½ cup olive oil
3 tablespoons lemon juice
1 egg
1 garlic clove
½ teaspoon salt
⅛ teaspoon pepper
    Pinch sugar
1 anchovy fillet, minced
½ cup garlic croutons
1 medium head romaine
    lettuce, torn
1 can (13 oz.) tuna, drained
    and flaked
¼ cup grated Parmesan
    cheese

In blender container combine oil, lemon juice, egg, garlic clove, salt, pepper and sugar; cover and blend until smooth. Stir in anchovy fillet. In large salad bowl combine romaine, tuna, Parmesan and dressing. Toss to coat greens. Add croutons and toss again lightly.

Polynesian Delight

1 quart pineapple sherbet
1 mango, sliced
1 banana, sliced
6 tablespoons canned crushed
    pineapple
8 tablespoons flaked coconut,
    toasted

Place 1 scoop sherbet in each of 4 parfait glasses; add a layer of sliced mango. Fill glass with more pineapple sherbet. Top with banana slices and crushed pineapple. Garnish with toasted coconut.

MAKE YOUR OWN CROUTONS

- Garlic Croutons: *Cut 3 slices firm bread into ½-inch cubes. In medium skillet heat ¼ cup olive oil. Add 2 crushed garlic cloves and cook 1 minute to flavor oil. Add bread cubes and brown on all sides, stirring occasionally. Cool.*
- Parmesan Cheese Croutons: *Saute 1 cup firm bread cubes in 4 tablespoons hot salad oil until golden brown. Transfer to paper towels with slotted spoon. Sprinkle lavishly with grated Parmesan cheese.*
- Easy Oven Croutons: *Spread firm bread cubes in single layer on ungreased baking sheet. Brown in 375° F. oven, stirring occasionally, for about 15 minutes.*

Maui Burgers

BURGERS WITH VEGETABLE-STUDDED RICE

Variations on the juicy hamburger are almost limitless. These beef patties are topped with pineapple slices and a sweet-and-sour sauce. Try the same sauce with pork chops some other day. The rice will cook while you prepare the burgers; total cooking time, about twenty minutes.

Menu for 4

- **Maui Burgers**   **Carrot Sticks**
  Plantain Chips **Coconut Cake**
- **Aloha Rice**

SHOPPING LIST

- ☐ 1 pound carrots
- ☐ 1 small green pepper
- ☐ 3 medium tomatoes
- ☐ 1 medium onion
- ☐ 1 bunch green onions
- ☐ 1 8-ounce can pineapple slices
- ☐ 1 package hamburger rolls
- ☐ 1 coconut cake
- ☐ 1 package plantain chips
- ☐ 1 pound ground beef

- ☐   Cornstarch
- ☐   Long-grain rice
- ☐   Salad oil
- ☐   Cider vinegar
- ☐   Chili sauce
- ☐   Soy sauce

Have on Hand

- ☐   Salt
- ☐   Ground ginger
- ☐   Sugar

SCHEDULE

1. Prepare carrot sticks; refrigerate to crisp.
2. Prepare Aloha Rice.
3. Prepare Maui Burgers.

Maui Burgers

Salt
1   pound ground beef
2   tablespoons salad oil
1   medium onion, sliced
1   small green pepper, sliced
1   can (8 oz.) pineapple
       slices
¼   cup cider vinegar
2   tablespoons sugar
2   tablespoons chili sauce
1   tablespoon soy sauce
¼   teaspoon ground ginger
1½ teaspoons cornstarch
       mixed with 1½ tea-
       spoons water
4   hamburger rolls

Sprinkle salt over bottom of heavy skillet. Heat skillet to very hot. Lower heat to medium, add patties and brown well on 1 side, about 5 minutes. Turn and cook 3 minutes more for medium rare to medium.

In large saucepan heat oil. Saute onion and pepper until onion is translucent. Drain syrup from pineapple into saucepan, reserving slices for burgers. Add remaining ingredients except rolls. Cook over medium heat, stirring until mixture comes to a boil. Boil 1 minute.

Place 1 burger on bottom half of each roll. Top with pineapple slice and ¼ cup sauce.

Aloha Rice

1¼ cups long-grain rice

1½ cups chopped tomatoes
½   cup chopped green onions
1   cup frozen green peas,
       thawed

Cook rice according to package directions. In serving bowl toss with chopped tomatoes, onions and thawed peas.

HAMBURGERS: TOP THEM WITH . . .

- *Pizza sauce, mozzarella cheese, anchovy fillets or pepperoni slices*
- *Lemon-sprinkled avocado chunks and sunflower seeds*
- *Soy-flavored stir-fried vegetables*
- *Cottage cheese, cucumber slices and fresh dill*
- *Crisp bacon and pineapple slices*
- *Leftover or canned chili and grated onion*
- *A sunny-side-up egg, a slice of American cheese and a splash of ketchup*
- *Pungent chutney and chopped peanuts*
- *Sauteed mushrooms and chopped green onions*
- *A generous slice of Monterey jack cheese and a spoonful of taco sauce*
- *Heated canned or frozen Oriental vegetables and crunchy Chinese noodles*
- *A thick slice of ripe tomato, red onion rings and crumbled bacon*

Taco Dogs

HOT WEATHER FOOD FROM SOUTH OF THE BORDER

Start this tasty meal with an easy and popular appetizer that gets its zing from jalapeño peppers. Heat the tacos and their filling while you're enjoying the nachos, and cool off after the meal with ice-cold watermelon.

Menu for 4

- **Nachos**
- **Taco Dogs**
- **Mexican Corn Salad**

Watermelon Slices

SHOPPING LIST

- ☐ 8 frankfurters
- ☐ 1 pound bacon
- ☐ 1 small head iceberg lettuce
- ☐ 1 medium tomato
- ☐ 1 red onion
- ☐ 1 pound carrots
- ☐ 1 bunch celery
- ☐ 1 wedge watermelon
- ☐ 1 10½-ounce can jalapeño bean dip
- ☐ 1 8-ounce jar mild taco sauce
- ☐ 1 jar sliced jalapeño peppers
- ☐ 1 4-ounce can chopped green chilies
- ☐ 1 10-ounce package frozen whole kernel corn
- ☐ 1 package tortilla chips
- ☐ 4 taco shells
- ☐ 1 8-ounce container sour cream
- ☐ 1 4-ounce package shredded cheddar cheese
- ☐ ¼ pound sliced Monterey jack cheese

Have on Hand
- ☐ Salt
- ☐ Pepper
- ☐ Sugar
- ☐ Salad oil
- ☐ Cider vinegar

SCHEDULE

1. Prepare Nachos.
2. Cook corn.
3. Prepare Taco Dogs.
4. Toss Mexican Corn Salad.

Nachos

1   can (10½ oz.) jalapeño
      bean dip
      Tortilla chips
¼   pound sliced Monterey
      jack cheese
      Sliced jalapeño peppers

Preheat oven to 350° F. Place ½ tablespoon bean dip on each tortilla chip; top with 1 piece of cheese and 1 pepper slice. Place chips on cookie sheet and heat in oven 10 minutes.

Taco Dogs

8   frankfurters, sliced in half
      lengthwise
1   jar (8 oz.) mild taco sauce
4   taco shells, heated
1   cup shredded Cheddar
      cheese
1   cup shredded lettuce
1   cup sour cream

In medium saucepan combine hot dogs and taco sauce; bring to a boil. Spoon into heated taco shells and top with cheese, lettuce and sour cream.

Mexican Corn Salad

1   package (10 oz.) frozen
      whole-kernel corn
1   medium tomato, chopped
⅓   cup chopped red onion
1   can (4 oz.) chopped green
      chilies, drained

Cook corn according to package directions; drain well. Transfer to serving dish and toss in remaining ingredients.

QUICK TACO ENTREES

For fast main dishes with a Mexican accent fill heated taco shells with:
- *canned chili and shredded Cheddar or Monterey jack cheese*
- *drained and chopped canned green chilies, refried beans and shredded cheese*
- *three-bean salad and ham or salami chunks*
- *warmed-up frankfurter slices and canned baked beans*
- *sliced cold cuts and deli cole slaw*
- *tuna or egg salad and avocado chunks*
- *leftover roast beef, shredded lettuce and red onion rings*
- *Sloppy Joe mixture and tomato chunks*

Shrimp Curry

SOUTH ASIAN SPECIALTIES

This curry, which takes little time to prepare, gets its tang from yogurt. Serve it on a bed of rice, with peanuts and mango chutney, the traditional condiment. Beer goes well with this meal.

Menu for 4

- **Shrimp Curry**
  Rice
- **Tossed Green**
  Salad with
  Peanut Butter
  Dressing

Peanuts
Mango
  Chutney
Sliced Papaya
  with Lime
  Wedges

SHOPPING LIST

- ☐ 1 pound medium shrimp
- ☐ 1 bunch celery
- ☐ 1 large onion
- ☐ 1 head leaf lettuce or other salad greens
- ☐ 1 ripe papaya
- ☐ 1 lime
- ☐ 1 small package shelled, unsalted, roasted peanuts
- ☐ 1 small jar mango chutney
- ☐ 1 8-ounce container plain yogurt

Have on Hand

- ☐ Salt
- ☐ Sugar
- ☐ Long-grain rice

- ☐ Butter or margarine
- ☐ Salad oil
- ☐ Cider vinegar
- ☐ Curry powder
- ☐ Peanut butter
- ☐ Soy sauce

SCHEDULE

1. Cook rice.
2. Prepare salad greens and Peanut Butter Dressing.
3. Prepare Shrimp Curry.
4. Toss salad.
5. Slice papaya.

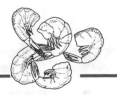

Shrimp Curry

¼ cup butter or margarine
1 cup chopped onions
1 to 2 tablespoons curry
    powder
1 pound medium shrimp,
    shelled and deveined
1 container (8 oz.) plain
    yogurt

In large skillet melt butter or margarine.
Add onions and curry powder; saute until
onions are translucent. Add shrimp; cook
just until shrimp turn pink. Add yogurt
and cook over low heat until hot, stirring
constantly. Serve with rice, peanuts and
mango chutney.

Tossed Salad with Peanut Butter Dressing

4 cups leaf lettuce or mixed
    salad greens
3 tablespoons peanut butter
3 tablespoons warm water

3 tablespoons salad oil
3 tablespoons soy sauce
2 teaspoons cider vinegar
2 teaspoons sugar

Tear greens into bite-size pieces and place
in large salad bowl. In large measuring
cup blend peanut butter and warm water.
Add remaining ingredients and mix well.
Toss with greens.

PEANUT BUTTER TIPS

• *Blend 1 tablespoon peanut butter
into ¼ cup yogurt; sweeten to taste
with honey and serve with a salad
of sliced bananas and walnuts.*
• *For a simple salad dressing, combine ½ cup oil, 2 tablespoons vinegar, a pinch of sugar, ground red
pepper to taste and 2 tablespoons
peanut butter.*
• *For a healthful snack, spread peanut butter on apple or pear chunks.*
• *Split bagels, spread with peanut
butter and top with banana slices.*
• *Thin 1 tablespoon peanut butter
with ½ teaspoon milk; stir into a
bowl of cream of chicken soup.*
• *To make a peanut butter milk
shake, add 1 tablespoon peanut
butter to 2 cups milk and 1 scoop
vanilla ice cream; whir in blender.*
• *For a tasty spread, mix peanut butter, grated onion and crumbled bacon; serve with crackers or rye
bread rounds.*

Seafood Pasta

SPAGHETTI WITH SCALLOPS AND TOMATO BREAD

Tiny, quick-cooking bay scallops and a bit of smoked salmon make this a satisfying and different pasta entree. The bread is flavored with fresh tomatoes and basil and the meal ends with creamy cheese and summer fruits (see Tips).

Menu for 4

- **Seafood Pasta**
- **Tomato Basil Bread**

Tossed Green Salad

Fruit and Cheese

SHOPPING LIST

- ½ pound bay scallops
- 1 ounce smoked salmon
- 1 8-ounce package thin spaghetti
- Salad greens
- 1 large tomato
- Fresh fruit
- 1 loaf French bread
- Cheese
- ½ pint heavy or whipping cream

- 1 bunch fresh basil or dried basil
- Garlic
- Bottled salad dressing
- Olive oil

Have on Hand
- Salt
- Pepper
- 1 bunch fresh dill or dillweed

SCHEDULE

1. Set cheese and fruit out to come to room temperature.
2. Heat water for spaghetti.
3. Prepare salad greens.
4. Prepare Tomato Basil Bread.
5. Prepare Seafood Pasta.

Seafood Pasta

1   *package (8 oz.) thin
        spaghetti*
½   *pound bay scallops*
1   *ounce smoked salmon, cut
        into ½-inch pieces*
¾   *cup heavy or whipping
        cream*
2   *garlic cloves, crushed*
¼   *teaspoon pepper*
⅛   *teaspoon salt*
2   *tablespoons chopped fresh
        dill or 1 teaspoon
        dillweed*

Cook spaghetti according to package directions. In medium saucepan combine all remaining ingredients except dill. Bring to a boil over medium-high heat. Reduce heat and simmer until scallops are done and sauce is slightly thickened, about 6 minutes. Drain spaghetti and toss with sauce. Garnish with chopped dill or dillweed.

Tomato Basil Bread

1   *loaf French bread*
1   *cup chopped tomato*
3   *tablespoons olive oil*
½   *teaspoon salt*
1   *tablespoon fresh basil or
        1½ teaspoons dried*
⅛   *teaspoon pepper*

Preheat broiler. Cut bread in half horizontally. In small bowl combine remaining ingredients; spread evenly on bread. Broil, cut side up, 8 to 10 minutes.

CHEESE-AND-FRUIT DESSERTS

The rich and creamy cheeses such as Brie and Camembert, which taste especially good with fresh fruits, are often served for dessert.

- *Always let them come to room temperature so that they will be runny at serving time.*
- *Other excellent dessert cheeses are Bel Paese, Creme Chantilly, Gervais and Boursin.*
- *The most popular fruit to serve with dessert cheeses are fresh pears, apples, cherries and seedless green grapes.*
- *For a special occasion sprinkle fresh raspberries with superfine sugar and serve with Petit Suisse.*
- *Dip seedless grapes in egg white and then in superfine sugar; serve with a triple cream cheese such as Saint-Andre.*
- *Those who love the blue cheeses will want to end an occasional meal with Stilton or Roquefort, fresh pears and walnut halves.*

Eggs McMuenster
A FAST-FOOD FAVORITE FOR HOME DINING

Ham, eggs and Muenster cheese on toasted English muffin halves—what could be tastier and more nourishing? Add a classic tossed salad and cool, delicious cherry pie for a meal no fast-food restaurant could compete with.

═══ Menu for 4 ═══

- **Eggs McMuenster**
- **Tossed Salad** **with Garlic Oil and Vinegar Dressing**

Cherry Pie

SHOPPING LIST

- ☐ ¼ pound Canadian bacon or ham in 4 slices
- ☐ 1 head romaine lettuce
- ☐ 1 green pepper
- ☐ 1 large tomato
- ☐ 1 bunch fresh basil or dried basil
- ☐ 1 10-ounce package frozen broccoli florets
- ☐ 4 English muffins
- ☐ 1 cherry pie
- ☐ ¼ pound sliced or shredded Muenster cheese
- ☐ 1 dozen eggs

Have on Hand
- ☐ Salt

- ☐ Pepper
- ☐ Sugar
- ☐ Garlic
- ☐ Butter or margarine
- ☐ Salad oil
- ☐ Red wine vinegar

SCHEDULE

1. Prepare salad and Garlic Dressing.
2. Prepare Eggs McMuenster.
3. Toss salad with dressing.

Eggs McMuenster

8   eggs
8   slices (8 oz.) Canadian
      bacon or ham
4   English muffins, split
¼   cup butter or margarine,
      divided
1   package (10 oz.) broccoli
      florets, cooked and drained
¼   pound Muenster cheese,
      sliced or shredded

Poach eggs. In large skillet cook bacon until lightly browned on both sides. Toast muffin halves; spread each with about ½ tablespoon butter or margarine. Place on broiler pan or cookie sheet.

Preheat broiler. Top each muffin half with bacon, broccoli, 1 poached egg and a scattering of cheese. Broil until cheese is slightly melted, 1 to 2 minutes.

Tossed Salad with Garlic Oil and Vinegar Dressing

1   head romaine lettuce, torn
1   large tomato, cut up
1   green pepper, cut up
½   cup salad oil
2   tablespoons plus 2 tea-
      spoons red wine vinegar
½   teaspoon salt
1   teaspoon chopped fresh
      basil or ¼ teaspoon dried
1   small garlic clove, crushed
      Dash sugar
      Dash pepper

In salad bowl combine lettuce, tomato and pepper chunks. In small jar with tight-fitting lid combine remaining ingredients; shake well. Toss salad with dressing at serving time.

ENGLISH MUFFIN MEALS

- **Niçoise on a Bun:** *Top cooled toasted muffin halves with flaked tuna, red onion rings, tomato chunks and hard-cooked egg slices.*
- **Pizza Muffin:** *Top toasted muffin halves with pizza sauce, grated mozzarella cheese, oregano and anchovy fillets.*
- **Eggs Benedict:** *On each buttered toasted muffin half place 1 slice sauteed ham or Canadian bacon and 1 poached egg; top with prepared hollandaise sauce.*
- **Bacon 'n' Peanut Butter Muffins:** *Spread peanut butter on hot toasted muffin halves and top with crisp bacon.*
- **Bacon, Sprouts and Tomato:** *Cover toasted muffin half with bean sprouts, tomato slices and crisp bacon and top with other half of muffin.*
- **Open-Face Grilled Cheese Sandwiches:** *Lay slices of American cheese on toasted muffin halves; top with any of the following— cooked asparagus spears or broccoli florets, tomato slices, sliced cooked ham or sausages, parboiled green pepper rings.*

Minted Lamb Chops

A SIMPLE BROILED ENTREE AND FROSTY DESSERT

Cook the chops in the broiler or on an outdoor grill. Add fresh yellow squash sauteed in butter, a creamy pea salad and a frosty coffee dessert drink. The result? A quick but satisfying warm weather meal.

═══ Menu for 4 ═══

- **Minted Lamb Chops**
- **Sauteed Summer Squash**
- **Garlic Bread**
- **Peas Pizzazz**
- **Alexander Icicles**

SHOPPING LIST

- ☐ 8   rib lamb chops
- ☐ 4   small summer squash
- ☐ 1   medium onion
- ☐ 1   bunch green onions
- ☐ 1   bunch fresh mint
- ☐ 1   10-ounce package frozen baby peas
- ☐ 1   8-ounce container sour cream
- ☐ 1   pint coffee ice cream
- ☐ ½   pint heavy or whipping cream or prepared whipped cream
- ☐   Creme de cacao
- ☐   Coffee bean candies (optional)

Have on Hand

- ☐   Salt
- ☐   Pepper
- ☐   Butter or margarine
- ☐   Bacon
- ☐   Brandy

SCHEDULE

1. Prepare Peas Pizzazz.
2. Saute summer squash.
3. Cook Minted Lamb Chops.
4. Prepare Alexander Icicles.

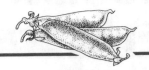

Minted Lamb Chops

8   rib lamb chops
1   teaspoon salt
1/4 teaspoon pepper
2   tablespoons chopped fresh
      mint
3   tablespoons minced onion

Preheat broiler or prepare grill. Sprinkle chops with salt, pepper, mint and onion. Broil or grill about 5 minutes on each side (depending on thickness) 3 inches from heat.

Garlic Bread

1/2 cup butter or margarine,
      softened
2   garlic cloves, minced
2   tablespoons chopped
      parsley
1   loaf baguette-style French
      bread

Preheat oven to 350° F. In small bowl thoroughly blend butter or margarine, garlic and parsley. Cut bread into thick slices, leaving bottom crust intact. Thinly spread cut surfaces with garlic butter. Press loaf back together and wrap loosely in foil, leaving top unsealed. Heat in oven 15 minutes.

Peas Pizzazz

1   package (10 oz.) frozen
      baby peas
1/2 cup sour cream
1   green onion, chopped
3   slices bacon, cooked and
      crumbled
1/4 teaspoon salt
1/8 teaspoon pepper

Thaw peas in cold water and drain well. Transfer to serving bowl; toss with remaining ingredients.

Alexander Icicles

1   pint coffee ice cream
2   tablespoons creme de cacao
2   tablespoons brandy
6   tablespoons sweetened
      whipped cream
    Coffee bean candies (optional)

Combine ice cream, creme de cacao and brandy in blender. Cover and whirl just until smooth and foamy. Pour into stemmed serving glasses and garnish with dollops of whipped cream and coffee bean candies.

Another Frosted Dessert Drink

• *For the children, prepare* Grape Apes: *In blender combine 1 pint vanilla ice cream and 1 cup grape juice. Whirl until smooth and foamy. Pour into stemmed glasses.*

Tomato and Cheese Frittata

PARMESAN-RICH EGGS

*This menu features a fluffy pancake-style omelet fla-
vored with Parmesan cheese and garnished with red,
ripe tomato slices. Vary the complementary fruit in
the blueberry dessert, if you wish; sliced peaches or
nectarines will taste delicious.*

Menu for 4

- **Tomato and Cheese Frittata**
- **Three-Bean Salad**
- **Garlic Bread**
- **Blueberries Chantilly**

SHOPPING LIST

- ☐ 1 dozen eggs
- ☐ 2 large, ripe tomatoes
- ☐ 1 large onion
- ☐ 1 16-ounce can small, whole potatoes
- ☐ 1 pint blueberries
- ☐ Orange and grapefruit sections or other fresh fruits
- ☐ 1 bunch parsley or basil
- ☐ 1 small can or package chopped walnuts (optional)
- ☐ 1 long loaf French bread
- ☐ 1 pound deli three-bean salad
- ☐ 1 8-ounce container sour cream
- ☐ ½ pint heavy or whipping cream or prepared whipped cream

Have on Hand

- ☐ Salt
- ☐ Pepper
- ☐ Garlic
- ☐ Butter or margarine
- ☐ Parmesan cheese

SCHEDULE

1. Mix topping and fruits for Blueberries Chantilly; chill separately.
2. Prepare Garlic Bread.
3. Cook Tomato and Cheese Frittata.

Tomato and Cheese Frittata

2   large ripe tomatoes, halved,
       seeded and sliced
     Salt
3   tablespoons butter or
       margarine
1   large onion, thinly sliced
       vertically
1   can (16 oz.) potatoes, diced
8   eggs, slightly beaten
6   tablespoons grated Parme-
       san cheese, divided
     Freshly ground pepper
2   or 3 tablespoons chopped
       parsley or basil

On large plate arrange tomato slices in single layer and sprinkle lightly with salt (this helps drain excess juices). Set aside.

In large heavy skillet melt butter or margarine. Add onion and saute until softened but not browned, about 8 minutes. Add potatoes and toss until coated; cook 1 minute. In large bowl whisk eggs with 4 tablespoons Parmesan, ¼ teaspoon salt and 12 twists pepper; pour into skillet and stir quickly. Reduce heat to medium-low, sprinkle on remaining cheese and let frittata settle, lifting edges to allow uncooked parts to run underneath. When frittata is firm, remove skillet from heat and sprinkle on parsley or basil. Arrange tomatoes on top. Serve at once or allow to cool in skillet and serve at room temperature.

Blueberries Chantilly

1½   cups blueberries
1½   cups orange and grape-
         fruit sections
½   cup sour cream
½   cup sweetened whipped
         cream
       Chopped walnuts
       (optional)

In serving bowl combine blueberries with orange and grapefruit sections; chill until serving time. In separate small bowl combine sour cream and whipped cream. Serve over fruit. Top with chopped nuts, if desired.

FAST FLAVORED BREADS

Slice a loaf of French bread almost through, leaving bottom crust intact. Spread with ¼ cup butter or margarine mixed with:

- *1 teaspoon lemon peel and 2 tablespoons parsley*
- *2 tablespoons toasted sesame, poppy or caraway seed*
- *2 tablespoons grated Parmesan cheese.*
- *Wrap loosely in foil and heat through in 350° F. oven.*

Philly Cheese Steaks

PROTEIN-PACKED HEROES

Made with quick-cooking sandwich steaks, these satisfying hero sandwiches are a meal in themselves. Team them with fresh green beans marinated in a tangy oil and vinegar dressing and served cold or at room temperature.

Menu for 4

- **Philly Cheese Steaks**
- **Green Bean Salad**
- **Strawberry Parfaits**

SHOPPING LIST

- ☐ 1   pound fresh green beans
- ☐ 5   medium onions
- ☐ 1   bunch fresh dill or dillweed
- ☐ ½   pint fresh strawberries
- ☐ 1   8-ounce package processed American cheese slices
- ☐ 4   6- to 8-inch hero rolls
- ☐ ½   pint heavy or whipping cream or prepared whipped cream
- ☐ 1   pint vanilla ice cream
- ☐ 1   pound frozen beef sandwich steaks

Have on Hand
- ☐   Salt

- ☐   Pepper
- ☐   Sugar
- ☐   Butter or margarine
- ☐   Salad oil
- ☐   Distilled white vinegar

SCHEDULE

1. Prepare Green Bean Salad; cover and refrigerate.
2. Prepare Philly Cheese Steaks.
3. Prepare Strawberry Parfaits.

Philly Cheese Steaks

3 tablespoons butter or
    margarine, divided
4 medium onions, thinly sliced
1 pound frozen beef sandwich
    steaks
4 hero rolls (6-8 in.), split
    lengthwise
6 slices processed American
    cheese, halved

In medium skillet melt 2 tablespoons butter or margarine over low heat. Add onions; saute slowly about 15 minutes.

Meanwhile, preheat oven to 425° F. Heat frozen steaks on jelly-roll pans or cookie sheet 4 to 5 minutes without turning. Spread cut sides of rolls with remaining 1 tablespoon butter. Wrap in foil and heat in oven 5 minutes. Unwrap rolls; fill with steaks, onions and cheese. Return to oven until cheese melts.

Green Bean Salad

1 pound fresh green beans
    Salt
1/3 cup finely chopped onion
1 tablespoon minced fresh
    dill or 1/2 teaspoon dillweed
1/2 cup water
1/4 cup distilled white vinegar
1 tablespoon sugar
    Dash pepper
2 tablespoons salad oil

In medium saucepan cook beans in salted water to cover until tender, about 10 minutes. Drain and plunge into cold water to cool; drain again. Combine in medium bowl with onion and dill.

In small jar with tight-fitting lid combine water, vinegar, sugar, 3/4 teaspoon salt, pepper and oil. Cover and shake. Pour over beans. Toss to coat. Cover and refrigerate until serving time.

Strawberry Parfaits

2 cups fresh strawberries
2 tablespoons sugar
1 pint vanilla ice cream
1 cup whipped cream

Place 4 parfait glasses in refrigerator to chill during meal. Set aside 4 large strawberries for garnish. Halve or quarter remaining strawberries; sprinkle with sugar and set aside. At serving time fill parfait glasses with alternating layers of ice cream, berries and whipped cream, ending with whipped cream. Top each parfait with a reserved strawberry.

THE PROCESSED CHEESES

Pasteurized processed cheeses are made by shredding and mixing fresh and aged natural cheeses. The result is a cheese with uniform flavor, body and texture and a long storage life. Use processed cheese for sandwiches, burger toppings, casseroles and snacks. Store wrapped in refrigerator.

Mozzarella in Carrozza

GRILLED SANDWICHES WITH ANCHOVY SAUCE

The Italian word carrozza *means "carriage," and in this sandwich entree the popular Neapolitan cheese arrives in a "carriage" made of Italian bread and accompanied by a garlic-flavored anchovy sauce. Serve the antipasto before or with the main course.*

Menu for 4

- **Antipasto Platter**
- **Mozzarella in Carrozza**

Fresh Pear Halves with Orange-Flavored Liqueur

SHOPPING LIST

- ☐ ¼   pound sliced salami
- ☐ 1   head lettuce
- ☐ 4   fresh pears
- ☐ 1   bunch fresh parsley
- ☐ 1   6-ounce jar marinated artichoke hearts
- ☐ 1   3¾-ounce jar marinated mushrooms
- ☐ 1   2-ounce can flat anchovy fillets
- ☐ 1   4-ounce jar roasted red peppers
- ☐ 1   small can ripe olives
- ☐ 1   large loaf Italian bread
- ☐ ½   pound mozzarella cheese

Have on Hand

- ☐   Milk
- ☐   Butter or margarine
- ☐   Eggs
- ☐   Garlic
- ☐   Olive oil
- ☐   Bottled Italian dressing
- ☐ 1   lemon or lemon juice
- ☐   Orange-flavored liqueur

SCHEDULE

1. Arrange Antipasto Platter.
2. Halve and core pears; top with orange-flavored liqueur.
3. Prepare Mozzarella in Carrozza.

Antipasto Platter

Lettuce leaves
1   jar (6 oz.) marinated arti-
    choke hearts, drained
1/4 pound salami slices, rolled
    into cylinders
12 ripe olives
1   jar (4 oz.) roasted red pep-
    pers, drained and cut
    into chunks
1   jar (3¾ oz.) marinated
    mushrooms
    Bottled Italian dressing

Line salad platter with lettuce leaves. Arrange remaining ingredients except dressing. Drizzle Italian dressing over all.

Mozzarella in Carrozza

1   can (2 oz.) flat anchovy
    fillets
1/4 cup olive oil
1   tablespoon lemon juice
1   garlic clove, crushed
8   slices large Italian bread
8   ounces mozzarella cheese,
    sliced
3   eggs
3   tablespoons milk
4   tablespoons butter or
    margarine
    Chopped parsley for
    garnish

In small saucepan combine anchovy fillets, olive oil, lemon juice and garlic
clove; crush with wooden spoon. Bring
to a boil, lower heat and simmer 5 minutes. Pour into blender and puree until
smooth; set aside.

Make sandwiches of bread and cheese.
In large shallow bowl beat eggs and milk.
In large heavy skillet over medium heat
melt butter or margarine. Dip each sandwich into egg mixture. Cook in skillet
about 3 minutes on each side or until
browned. Sprinkle with parsley and serve
with warm anchovy sauce.

MOZZARELLA SNACKS

- *Cut thick slices of bread into quarters, remove crusts and make small
  mozzarella sandwiches. Dip in
  beaten egg diluted with a little
  milk. Fry in hot oil until golden.*
- *Thread chunks of bread and equal-
  sized slices of mozzarella on
  wooden skewers; broil until cheese
  is melted and bread is toasted.*
- *Wrap chunks of mozzarella with
  strips of thinly sliced boiled ham,
  prosciutto or salami. Secure with
  toothpicks.*
- *Spear small cherry tomatoes and
  small cubes of mozzarella one-and-
  one on toothpicks.*

Elena Ruz

EXTRA-QUICK MAIN-DISH SANDWICH

Here is a meal the children will love. It requires almost no cooking and very little, if any, shopping; you'll probably find most of the ingredients on your kitchen shelves or in your refrigerator. Add sliced bananas to the salad, if you wish, or garnish with mandarin orange sections.

Menu for 4

- **Elena Ruz**
- **Apple, Grape and Celery Salad**
- **Chocolate Crumb Parfaits**

SHOPPING LIST

- ☐ ½ pound sliced cooked turkey breast
- ☐ 1 bunch celery
- ☐ 1 head lettuce
- ☐ 4 large red apples
- ☐ 1 bunch seedless grapes
- ☐ 1 lemon
- ☐ 1 small can or package chopped walnuts
- ☐ 1 regular size package instant chocolate pudding
- ☐ 1 loaf white bread
- ☐ 1 3-ounce package cream cheese

Have on Hand
- ☐ Salt

- ☐ Paprika
- ☐ Sugar
- ☐ Butter or margarine
- ☐ Mayonnaise
- ☐ Graham cracker crumbs
- ☐ Strawberry jam or preserves
- ☐ Uncooked oats or granola

SCHEDULE

1. Prepare Chocolate Crumb Parfaits; refrigerate.
2. Prepare Apple, Grape and Celery Salad.
3. Prepare Elena Ruz.

Elena Ruz

8   slices white bread
1   package (3 oz.) cream
      cheese, softened
½   pound sliced cooked turkey
      breast
6   tablespoons strawberry jam
      or preserves

Spread 4 slices bread with cream cheese. Top with turkey. Spread remaining bread with jam or preserves and place, jam side down, over turkey. Place on hot ungreased griddle or skillet and grill until golden brown on both sides, pressing down with pancake turner on each side.

Apple, Grape and Celery Salad

4   large red apples
3   ribs celery, chopped
⅓   cup halved seedless grapes
¼   cup chopped walnuts
3   tablespoons mayonnaise
1   teaspoon lemon juice
½   teaspoon grated lemon
      peel
      Pinch sugar
      Pinch salt
      Lettuce leaves
      Grapes for garnish

Core and cube apples; do not peel. In large bowl combine apples, celery, grapes and nuts. In small bowl mix mayonnaise, lemon juice and peel, sugar and salt. Fold dressing into fruit and nuts. Serve on lettuce leaves. Garnish with grapes.

Chocolate Crumb Parfaits

2   tablespoons butter or
      margarine, melted
½   cup graham cracker
      crumbs
2   tablespoons uncooked oats
      or granola
1   tablespoon sugar
1   package (regular size) in-
      stant chocolate pudding

Combine melted butter or margarine with cracker crumbs, oats or granola and sugar. Prepare chocolate pudding according to package directions. Layer pudding and crumbs in 4 parfait glasses.

FRUIT SALAD TIP

• *Dress orange sections, grapes and walnuts with a well-blended mixture of 1 container (8 oz.) plain yogurt, 2 tablespoons each orange and lemon juice and 1 tablespoon honey.*

Reuben Sandwiches

CORNED BEEF ON RYE WITH MELTED CHEESE

Serve this popular sandwich on one of those nippy end-of-summer days when you're short of time and energy. Vary the Saucy Fruit Cake by substituting seasonal fruits or thawed frozen mixed fruit and flavored brandy.

═══ Menu for 4 ═══

- **Reuben Sandwiches Potato Salad**
- **Cucumber-Onion Salad**
- **Saucy Fruit Cake**

SHOPPING LIST

- ☐ ¾ pound thinly sliced corned beef
- ☐ 2 medium cucumbers
- ☐ 1 bunch green onions
- ☐ 2 peaches or nectarines
- ☐ 1 pint blueberries or strawberries
- ☐ 1 small bunch seedless grapes
- ☐ 1 16-ounce can or package sauerkraut
- ☐ 1 loaf rye bread
- ☐ 1 pound cake
- ☐ 4 ounces sliced Swiss cheese
- ☐ 1 pound deli potato salad
- ☐ 1 pint vanilla ice cream

Have on Hand
- ☐ Salt

- ☐ Pepper
- ☐ Sugar
- ☐ Butter or margarine
- ☐ White vinegar
- ☐ Red pepper sauce
- ☐ Bottled Russian dressing
- ☐ Brandy

SCHEDULE

1. Slice and combine fruit for dessert; add brandy and chill.
2. Prepare Cucumber-Onion Salad.
3. Prepare Reuben Sandwiches.
4. Toast pound cake and assemble dessert.

Reuben Sandwiches

4 slices rye bread
2 tablespoons butter or
   margarine
4 tablespoons bottled Russian dressing
¾ pound cooked thinly sliced
   corned beef
2 cups sauerkraut, rinsed
   and drained
4 slices (4 oz.) Swiss cheese

Preheat oven to 350° F. Lightly toast rye bread; spread one side with butter or margarine. Spread 1 tablespoon Russian dressing on each slice. Layer corned beef and sauerkraut and top with cheese slices. Place on cookie sheet and bake 10 to 14 minutes.

Cucumber-Onion Salad

2 medium cucumbers,
   peeled, seeded and sliced
2 green onions, sliced
½ teaspoon salt
1 teaspoon sugar
1 tablespoon white vinegar
   Dash red pepper sauce

In medium bowl toss cucumbers with green onions, salt, sugar, vinegar and red pepper sauce; toss well. Set aside for 10 minutes. Toss lightly before serving.

Saucy Fruit Cake

2 large peaches or nectarines, peeled, pitted and
   sliced
1 cup blueberries or sliced
   strawberries
1 cup halved seedless grapes
2 tablespoons brandy
½ pound cake
1 pint vanilla ice cream

In medium bowl combine fruit with brandy. Cut cake into 4 slices; toast slices until golden brown. Top each slice with 1 scoop ice cream. Spoon on brandied fruit sauce.

POTATO SALAD TIPS

Dress up 1 pound deli potato salad by adding:
* *¼ cup chopped pimiento-stuffed green olives*
* *2 tablespoons grated onion*
* *½ cup chopped fresh tomato*
* *½ cup ham cubes*
* *¼ cup chopped green pepper*

Riviera Tuna and Bean Salad

NO-COOK MAIN DISH WITH BLENDER SOUP

This delightful summer soup is similar to gazpacho. Vary the seasonings to suit your own taste. The tuna salad is made with fresh green beans, but you can toss it together with deli three-bean salad.

Menu for 4

- **Cold Fresh Tomato Soup**
- **Riviera Tuna and Bean Salad**

Rye Bread with Butter

Lemon Ice with Chilled Vodka

SHOPPING LIST

- ☐ 1 13-ounce can tuna
- ☐ 6 medium tomatoes
- ☐ 1 small onion
- ☐ 1 pound fresh green beans
- ☐ 2 or 3 lemons or lemon juice
- ☐ 1 loaf rye bread
- ☐ 1 8-ounce container sour cream
- ☐ 1 pint lemon ice

- ☐ Salad oil
- ☐ Tarragon vinegar
- ☐ Red pepper sauce
- ☐ Dijon mustard
- ☐ Anchovy paste
- ☐ Vodka

Have on Hand
- ☐ Salt
- ☐ Pepper
- ☐ Curry powder
- ☐ Butter or margarine
- ☐ Garlic
- ☐ Olive oil

SCHEDULE

1. Place vodka in freezer to chill.
2. Prepare Cold Fresh Tomato Soup; refrigerate.
3. Prepare Riviera Tuna and Bean Salad.

Cold Fresh Tomato Soup

6   *medium tomatoes*
1   *quart boiling water*
2   *teaspoons minced onion*
¼   *cup fresh lemon juice*
¼   *cup salad oil*
1   *teaspoon salt*
    Dash pepper
3   *drops red pepper sauce*
¼   *teaspoon curry powder*
½   *cup sour cream*

Dip tomatoes in boiling water for about 10 seconds; use tip of paring knife to slip off skin. Halve tomatoes, squeeze out and discard seeds and cut into chunks. Puree tomatoes and onion in blender at medium speed. Transfer to large bowl. Add remaining ingredients except sour cream; chill until serving time. Serve in bowls garnished with sour cream.

Riviera Tuna and Bean Salad

1   *pound fresh green beans,*
    trimmed
2   *tablespoons tarragon*
    vinegar
1   *teaspoon Dijon mustard*
1   *teaspoon anchovy paste*
1   *garlic clove, crushed*
3   *tablespoons olive oil*
3   *tablespoons salad oil*

1   *can (13 oz.) tuna, drained*
    and broken into bite-sized
    chunks

In medium saucepan cook beans in salted water to cover about 10 minutes, until tender. Drain and plunge into cold water to cool; drain well.

In small jar with tight-fitting lid combine vinegar, mustard, anchovy paste, garlic and oils; shake well. Arrange beans and tuna on serving platter and sprinkle dressing on top, or combine beans and tuna in salad bowl and toss with dressing.

QUICK ZING WITH RED PEPPER SAUCE

- *Splash a few drops of bottled red pepper sauce into packaged corn bread mix for instant flavor.*
- *Use in place of dried hot peppers in fiery Mexican or Szechuan cooking.*
- *Add ¼ teaspoon to 1 pound of ground beef to put bite into your burgers.*
- *Put a drop or two into white sauce or curry sauce for fast spice.*

Sauteed Chicken with Blueberry Sauce

CHICKEN WITH A TOUCH OF FRUIT

This unusual entree is special enough to serve to guests or at a party, yet simple enough to toss together for a quick family meal. Stir some grated orange peel into the rice to complement the chicken sauce, if you wish.

Menu for 4

- **Sauteed Chicken with Blueberry Sauce Rice**
- **Zucchini with Onion and Garlic**
- **Gold Digger Sundaes**

SHOPPING LIST

- ☐ 4 chicken cutlets
- ☐ 4 small zucchini
- ☐ 1 small onion
- ☐ 1 pint blueberries
- ☐ 2 bananas
- ☐ 1 pint butter pecan ice cream
- ☐ 1 small can or package pecan halves
- ☐ 1 small jar butterscotch topping

Have on Hand
- ☐ Cornstarch
- ☐ Long-grain rice
- ☐ Salt
- ☐ Pepper

- ☐ Garlic
- ☐ Butter or margarine
- ☐ Salad oil
- ☐ Orange juice
- ☐ Orange-flavored liqueur

SCHEDULE

1. Cook rice.
2. Prepare Sauteed Chicken with Blueberry Sauce.
3. Saute Zucchini with Onion and Garlic.
4. Prepare Gold Digger Sundaes.

Sauteed Chicken with Blueberry Sauce

4 chicken cutlets
½ teaspoon salt
⅛ teaspoon pepper
2 tablespoons butter or margarine
1 teaspoon minced garlic
1½ cups orange juice
1 tablespoon cornstarch dissolved in ¼ cup orange-flavored liqueur
1 cup blueberries

Season chicken with salt and pepper. In heavy skillet heat butter or margarine. Add chicken and garlic; saute 3 minutes on each side; transfer to serving platter. To same skillet add orange juice and cornstarch mixture. Stir until thickened; cook 1 minute. Add chicken and blueberries. Simmer 5 minutes more.

Zucchini with Onion and Garlic

2 tablespoons butter or margarine
2 tablespoons salad oil
2 tablespoons grated onion
1 small garlic clove, crushed
4 small zucchini, trimmed and halved lengthwise
½ teaspoon salt
⅛ teaspoon pepper
2 tablespoons water

In large skillet heat butter or margarine and salad oil over medium heat. Add onion and garlic, lower heat and cook 3 minutes. Season zucchini halves with salt and pepper; add to skillet, cut side down, and cook until golden. Turn zucchini, add water to skillet. Cook uncovered over low heat about 5 minutes or until just tender.

Gold Digger Sundaes

1 pint butter pecan ice cream
2 bananas, sliced
½ cup pecan halves
½ cup butterscotch topping, divided

Place 1 scoop ice cream in each of 4 dessert dishes. Top each with banana slices, pecan halves and 2 tablespoons butterscotch topping.

RICE TIPS

- *Store uncooked rice at room temperature in a clean, dry container; it will keep almost indefinitely. After cooking, store covered in refrigerator 4 to 5 days.*
- *To reheat, place in covered saucepan; add 2 tablespoons liquid for each cup of rice. Simmer 4 to 5 minutes. Or cover and heat in microwave 1 to 2 minutes.*
- *Cooked rice can be frozen and kept for 6 to 8 months. Thaw before reheating.*

Index

For information on how to subscribe to
Ladies' Home Journal, please write to:

Ladies' Home Journal
Box 10895
Des Moines, IA 50336-0895